SHADOWS OF IMMORTALITY

*Untold Struggles of
Henrietta Lacks' Grandson*

Alfred (Lacks) Carter, Jr.

SHADOWS OF IMMORTALITY
Alfred (Lacks) Carter, Jr

All rights reserved. No portion of this book may be reproduced, scanned, stored in a retrieval system, transmitted in any form or by any means – electronically, mechanically, photocopy, recording or any other – except for brief quotations in printed reviews, without the written permission of the publisher. Please do not participate in or encourage piracy of copyrighted materials in violation of the author's rights. Purchase on authorized editions.

Copy and Content Editing Anthony KaDarrell Thigpen of Literacy in Motion

www.LiteracyinMotion.Ink

Library of Congress Cataloging-in-Publication Data
ISBN: 9798871066867

SHADOWS OF IMMORTALITY
Untold Struggles of Henrietta Lacks' Grandson

Biographies/ Memoirs
Printed in the United States of America

SHADOWS OF IMMORTALITY | *Alfred (Lacks) Carter, Jr.*

Honoring
HENRIETTA LACKS
August 1, 1920 -to- October 4, 1951

Emerging from the shadows of his grandmother's immortal legacy, Alfred (Lacks) Carter, Jr., unveils a captivating autobiography, revealing a life scarred by socioeconomic despair and childhood trauma. His journey takes us through a harrowing descent into drug addiction, criminal entanglements, and the depths of infidelity, culminating in a 30-year prison sentence.

Yet, amidst the darkness, a glimmer of hope emerges. Inspired by his grandmother, Henrietta Lacks, whose groundbreaking HeLa cells revolutionized medical research, Alfred embarks on a path of redemption. His story is a testament to the indomitable human spirit, a beacon of hope for those trapped in cycles of despair.

Through his debut memoir, Alfred shatters the chains of silence, exposing the societal pitfalls faced by marginalized communities. He unveils the exploitation endured by Henrietta Lacks' descendants, while simultaneously celebrating their resilience and unwavering determination to triumph over life's adversities.

In the Shadows of Immortality is a poignant tale of transformation, a testament to the power of legacy and the enduring strength of the human spirit. Join Alfred on this extraordinary journey as he confronts his past, embraces redemption, and emerges as a champion for the marginalized.

The Authentic Signature of Henrietta Lacks.

DEDICATION

In Honor Of
Deborah Jean Lacks

This book is dedicated to my mom, Deborah Jean Lacks, for inspiring many, especially myself. She was always a tremendous support, even during life's most challenging seasons. During triumphs and tragedies, my mom's dedication and determination proved exceptional. She died during her quest to uncover the truth about her mother, the unsung hero of the immortal HeLa cells. As a result, her compassion has inspired me to continue her work of telling the world our story - we are the proud descendants of Henrietta Lacks.

TABLE OF CONTENT

Introduction,   pg. 7
EXPLOITATED

Chapter 1,   pg. 23
DESPERATION

Chapter 2,   pg. 28
DEBORAH'S QUEST

Chapter 3,   pg. 40
REMINSCING

Chapter 4,   pg. 47
LIFE'S ROLLERCOASTER

Chapter 5,   pg. 65
NO QUICK FIX

Chapter 6,   pg. 73
A NEW BEGINNING

Chapter 7,   pg. 91
ABSENT FROM GOD'S PRESENCE

Chapter 8,   pg. 99
FROM BOYS TO MEN

Chapter 9,   pg. 107
JUSTICE FOR ALL

Chapter 10,   pg. 116
CATCH ME IF YOU CAN

Chapter 11,   pg. 133
THE IMMORTAL TRIUMPH

INTRODUCTION
EXPLOITATED

It all began, **October 4, 1951,** when scientist realized they could make history and lots of money off the immortal cells of Henrietta Lacks. Allegedly buried in an unknown grave in 1951, the story of my grandmother, Henrietta Lacks, is often lost in the shadows.

Henrietta Lacks was buried between her mom, Eliza Pleasant and her oldest daughter, Elsie Lacks. Like many other tales written about Grandma Henrietta, the myth of her unknown burial site is also untrue. It was always known by family and friends that my grandmother was buried between her mom and daughter in an unmarked grave, but not an unknown site.

My mother, Deborah Lacks, spent her life digging for the truth. Unfortunately, she died 9 months before the release of the book, "The Immortal Life of Henrietta Lacks." Rebecca Skloot took all the credit. There was no mention of my mother's tireless contribution or payment to her estate for the publication. My personal story weaves in-and-out the shadows of Grandma Henrietta's legacy – this is my story.

Sometimes, life gets out of whack, and nothing happens in the sequence we hoped. Some people die way too soon. Divorces spiral unexpectedly. Bitterness, hate, pain, and deception make the shadows even darker. It can almost make you feel delusional, searching and facing truths born in tragedy.

Time moves so fast that memories get mixed together. One thing is sure: countless money-hungry scavengers disguised in sheep's clothing have sought to ravish my family's legacy.

Unfortunately, my life spiraled through twists and turns, and I found myself viewing reality from inside prison bars for 15 years. I survived through the love of my mother and son; their visits, my memories, and our family legacy kept me alive. Now, the world will know that my mother did not dedicate her life in vain. Her discoveries did not merely uncover hidden truths but led to justice for the descendants of Henrietta Lacks.

Before activist Dick Gregory died, he spoke candidly to me face to face. "Write your own book and tell your own story," he said. He also made other passionately vulgar comments about those who misused my family for selfish gain. I dare not repeat them, but he inspired me. So, I'm standing on the shoulders of giants like Mr. Gregory, my mom, Deborah Lacks, the woman who played her character in the HBO film Oprah Winfrey, and ultimately my grandmother, Henrietta Lacks.

The legendary Mr. Dick Gregory and Alfred (Lacks) Carter at the Hyatt Regency lobby in Atlanta, Georgia in 2016.

Oprah in Baltimore at the four seasons hotel in 2017.

Marginalized people seldom get the opportunity to tell their stories from their own perspectives. Either we must water down our victories, exaggerate our tribulations with sensationalism, or sugarcoat the truth to be heard. But I'm determined to speak my whole truth while standing in the shadows because extraordinary people often survive life's darkest challenges. Though darkness may surround me, I've discovered a comforting truth: where there's no flicker of light, shadows cannot exist. This revelation, a childhood gift tucked deep within my heart, has become an unyielding beacon of hope, a luminescent thread guiding me through even the darkest nights.

During the 1960's and 70's, urban cities across America were plagued with poverty, racism, and discrimination. The economic landscape of urban cities was defined by welfare food stamps and government food lines with boxed cheese. Countless families remained trapped in this vicious cycle as victims of inequality.

Dilapidated neighborhoods, failing schools, and liquor stores displaced throughout every community created a trap we could not all easily escape then or now. Extreme unjust incarcerations of Black men, a mysterious influx of unlawful weapons, illegal drug trafficking, drugs addicts, and prostitution started diminishing our trust in the police, the legal system, and the government.

Quite frankly, many of us felt like white people were the enemy aiming to annihilate Black people. For decades, a strong message was sent by those in authority that Black lives don't matter. In neighborhoods surrounded by invisible walls of impoverishment, victimization occurs. It's not unusual to see struggling single mothers, absent fathers, domestic abuse, neglect, and churches peddling hope for funds instead of evangelizing Christ for salvation. As a result of isolated success stories, the collective masses are accused of being lazy, unmotivated, or the cause of their own shame, suffering, and struggles. Marginalized people are belittled, devalued, and overlooked. Far too many are left behind. This book, **SHADOWS OF IMMORTALITY**, gives voice to struggling brothers and sisters that are waiting to walk into the light.

A poverty mentality is often rooted in fear. The fear of stepping outside our comfort zone, facing psychological challenges, and dealing with the emotional embers from our past. Many triumphant family stories go untold because our tragedies keep them sealed in secrecy. Fear forces marginalized people to retreat in silence instead of charging by faith. I am compelled to hurdle over the pitfalls of my past and leap into the light.

In 2016, I started doing speaking engagements at various universities and institutions with Skloot, and a few of my cousins. It was 2017 when the book *The Immortal Life of Henrietta Lacks* became an HBO film.

I did the speaking engagements initially because I was in desperate needs of money to support myself. As audiences asked questions about the book, the more I recognized Rebecca's agenda did not align with our family's best interests.

That's when I knew it was essential to re-tell portions of our story from the first-person perspective of Henrietta Lack's descendants. Unfortunately, my decision to stop speaking to promote the book did not prevent a few other family members from doing so. When people are desperate for money and have unmet needs, they'll compromise a lot to get it, and understandably so. Even still, Rebecca's book and the movie, allegedly based on my family, had a lot of embellishments.

Oprah and Alfred (Lacks) Carter, Jr. on the set of "The Immortal Life of Henrietta Lacks" in Fells Point, Baltimore in 2017.

I'm forever grateful that Oprah Winfrey convinced the directors to script a speaking part for me in the movie. I was privileged to see a pre-screening of the overall production with Oprah. After watching the full film, and processing how my family was portrayed, I started embracing the need to tell my own story. I am grateful for the exposure we received, but truth and justice always prevail over glitz and glamour.

I understand the need for made-for-TV accommodations, but the book failed to expose my family's rich qualities, strong heritage, and undying loyalty. We are not ignorant, backwoods, or immoral. We simply come from a culture and community that Rebecca was unable to capture with her pen or embrace with her heart. And yes, many of the Lacks descendants have made mistakes, but those bad choices do not define us. In some instances, we did not know any other way of life, and it takes a lot of courage to reform one's reality.

Rebecca knew the science behind HeLa cells but failed to recognize the dignity of my grandmother's descendants. Therefore, she took our story, made it her own, and justified herself to the world by convincing others that we were deplorables. She paid a select group of family members to speak at various events. Our job was to answer audience questions and describe snapshots of our past. She paid us peanuts and drifted into the shadows as a stranger and millionaire.

Rebecca misused my mother's deepest passions and family treasures and journaled about our tragedies but overlooked our triumphs. She portrayed our personal, family, and religious experiences in the shadows of negativity nuances, instead of strength and pride.

Her influence created chaos and division within our family because some praised the ground Rebecca walked on. Others knew that she cared nothing about our struggles. She deceived us, pretending to care, only to strip away our family secrets.

Some of my struggling cousins remained accepting as long as Rebecca continued dangling small carrots of revenue. We continued living in the shadows, and she got rich. Rebecca used my cousin Jeri Lacks to rally family members to form an alliance against my Uncle Lawrence and my cousin Ron. However, I love my cousin Jeri and refuse to judge her decisions. I didn't like it, but I understand people have a right to make their own choices.

Contrary to the book, my grandmother made choices about her life that were poorly illustrated in Rebecca's portrayal. Henrietta Lacks was not a poor Black tobacco farmer; she was the loving and faithful wife of my hard-working grandfather. The narrative used to paint the backdrop of my family story was reminiscent of agricultural impoverishment. Rebecca used her literary finesse to push us deeper into the shadows.

Our true story was buried alive and left in Rebecca's imaginary unmarked grave. As another example, my mother, Deborah Lacks, was not insane, violent, or delusional. She was a licensed hair stylist and barber. She was emotional and in despair. Deborah lost her mom at age 2 and spent a lifetime in the shadows chasing the ghost of my grandmother's immortality.

As another ploy of sensationalism, Rebecca told the world that I received my GED in prison. She didn't get that information from my proud mother, who attended my High School graduation. I sometimes wonder if her false narratives served the purpose of painting an Anglo-Saxon portrayal of Black history. There was no mention of me enlisting in the Marines to serve my country immediately afterward. That would make the Lacks descendants look too patriotic. Instead, we were portrayed as back wood negroes who knew nothing about modern civilization.

Alfred Carter, Jr. and my cousin Jeri Lacks attending the Red-Carpet event in New York City for the movie premiere of The Immortal life of Henrietta Lacks in Manhattan, April 18, 2017.

Alfred (Lacks) Carter, Jr. USMC boot camp graduation, 3rd Battalion H Company, Platoon 3076, Parris Island, South Carolina, September 1984.

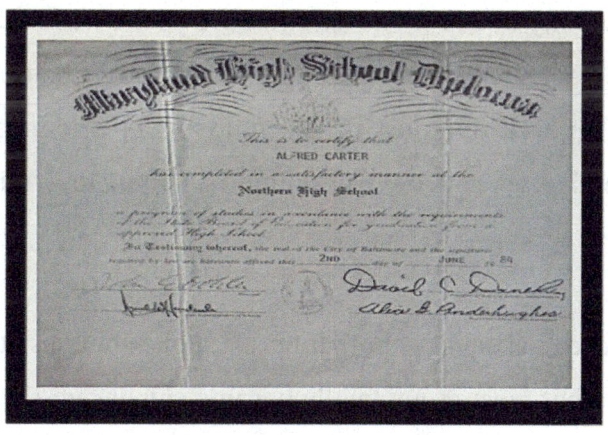

Alfred (Lacks) Carter, Jr. Maryland High School graduation diploma, June 1984.

Although it served as a great scientific read that raised awareness about my grandmother's HeLa cells, her characterizations did a disservice to our family. The book and movie made Rebecca lots of money, but it demanded no justice for my family.

When my mother passed away, and my son was murdered, Rebecca was contacted both times. She failed to send flowers or condolences, and she did not attend. Even worse, we asked Rebecca, as the founding representative of the Henrietta Lacks Foundation, to assist with my son's burial. She did not. The last time I saw Rebecca was at a speaking engagement at Stanford University in 2018. The last time we spoke was in 2020, when my son was murdered on the streets of Baltimore. She ignored our plea to use funds from a foundation named after my own grandmother to help with the burial.

Rebecca's absence at both funerals spoke volumes. It was then that most of my family became convinced; she was the first of many who came to ravish our family's memories and liquidate our legacy. She took total credit for writing *The Immortal Life of Henrietta Lacks* well over 10 years ago. With the use of paid speaking engagements, she is still trying to usurp authority over my family's legacy as we move forward. I always say it's her slave-owner mentality. She does not seem to realize we are not in chains – Rebecca will not let go of the noose around the neck of Henrietta Lacks' family legacy.

My aunts and uncles have all passed away: Lawrence, Elsie, Sonny, Deborah, and Joe. Lawrence lived for justice and was the last to die on August 26, 2023, twenty-four days after we won our first settlement on behalf of my grandmother. Thanks to help of attorney Ben Crump and his team of attorneys, along with Professor Deleso Alford and attorneys Nigel Halliday, Chris Ayers, Chris Seeger, and Kim Parker we are now focused on the living legacy Henrietta Lacks.

This legacy is our victory cry for marginalized people. Aside from Johns Hopkins Hospital, Rebecca was the first of many who used the Lacks legacy for selfish gain and left us empty-handed. Nonetheless, we press forward. I'm thankful that Rebecca fueled my passion to speak truth to power and to be a voice preventing marginalized people from being exploited.

"Shadows of Immortality," is my personal story as the grandson of Henrietta Lacks. My mom passed away while I sat in prison in 2009 – it was the second time I cried uncontrollably – yet I was unable to properly grieve. Nine months later, the book that took from the core of her soul, was released solely in the name of Rebecca Skloot. Instead of allowing others to liquidate our legacy through exploitation, I am telling my story. It is pastime that the Lacks legacy comes out of the shadows into the marvelous light.

Chapter 1

DESPERATION

It was 7:43 p.m. on **January 26, 2001**, as Eric and I sat in my forest green 1997 Toyota, Avalon across the street from the liquor store. The corner store also cashed checks which made it the perfect spot for us to burglarize, so we thought.

I finished smoking by taking one last long pull from the Newport cigarette. As I exhaled a thick cloud of smoke, I looked at Eric and asked, "You ready?" He replied, "Yea, let's get this money." I reached under my driver seat, grabbed my nickel-plated 38 caliber with the pearl handle, and put it in my waistband. Eric and I got out the car and started casually walking toward the liquor store. Reaching the front door, I walked in as Eric followed immediately on my heels.

The store cashed checks daily, so we were convinced we'd come-up once the job was done. The store had two customers, but Eric and I always made it happen, no matter who was inside. Eric walked towards the back of the store to keep the male worker in check. I went straight toward the lady that was close to the safe.

I terrorized the woman by immediately whipping out my gun. While pointing it at her, I said, "Don't make any sudden moves lady, just open the safe." As she bent down to open the safe, I quickly leaped over the counter before she even knew what happened behind her. With one hand removing the cash from the safe and the other pointing my 38 pistol at the cashier, I moved skillfully and swiftly.

As the frightened lady laid face down on the floor, I heard a loud disturbance from Eric's direction. I looked up and saw Eric and the male employee wrestling for a gun. Somehow, Eric was caught off guard and found himself in a violent tussle.

They both lost their balance, stumbling to the floor and falling apart from one another's grip. During this sudden separation, the worker grabbed Eric's gun and started pointing it in Eric direction. Eric ran! As he pointed his gun at Eric's back, all I could see was my friend running toward me for his life. I pointed my gun in the man's general direction and squeezed off 3 shots as a distraction so that we could escape.

The male worker scrambled for safety, diving behind the counter to save his life. Eric and I ran out of the store making a straight shot toward my car for a quick getaway. After jumping in the car, we were both nervous and shaking from the unexpected adrenalin rush of having to result to suppress rounds to escape the scene. While speeding from the liquor store, a Baltimore police car suddenly appeared behind us with flashing lights and a loud siren. Eric looked back, saying, "What the fuck!". I replied, "I'm about to dust his ass because we are not going to jail tonight!" I had to shake the cops quickly before backup arrived to assist him.

Drastic times called for drastic measures. We blasted the album lyrics to hip hop gangsta rapper, Tupac Shakur, "Until the End of Time" and started out racing the cops. I went down a one-way street, hopped the curb, made a left down an alley, and once we were on a main street, I floored my Toyota Avalon to make our great escape. We got away! Once we were out of the vicinity, I brought the car to an easy chill to avoid stirring unwanted attention. Eric said, "Damn, that was close." I replied, "Shit, you know I'm a driving motherfucker. I told you we weren't going to jail tonight." We immediately gave each other a fist bump as Eric said, "Let's go get high."

Getting high is how we medicated ourselves to cope with all the mental chaos of struggling and hustling in the hood. It's a series of life events that led to this day of desperation, and for me, it all started during my childhood.

Chapter 2
DEBORAH'S QUEST

It was 5:03 a.m. on **November 10, 1966,** when I was born in the Baltimore City Hospital. My mother is Deborah Jean Lacks, and I am the oldest of two children. My sister, LaTonya, is 4 years younger than me. Baltimore, known for its shipyards and thriving steel mills, was a blue-collar town with middle-class money to be made by black men such as my dad.

My beautiful mom, Deborah Lacks, at the age of 23 in Baltimore, Maryland.

The insidious grip of drugs and alcohol tightened around Black communities in the late 1960s, leaving a trail of shattered lives and fractured families. Under the shroud of addiction, the once vibrant hues of daily life turned into shades of despair.

My own father, caught in the tempest of substance abuse, succumbed to alcoholism and drug addiction, transforming our home into a battleground. The fists of violence, fueled by drugs and alcohol, rained down upon my mother, Deborah, leaving her spirit battered and bruised.

In the face of this harrowing reality, my young and impressionable mind yearned for an escape, a refuge from the chaos that surrounded me. The desperation for a better life intensified with each passing day, gnawing at my soul. While I own up to the mistakes I've made, the inescapable exposure to this destructive lifestyle would lay the foundation for my own struggle with addiction.

I must have been no more than 4 years old when my mind captured my first lifelong memory of my father's addiction. My dad, Alfred Sr., was nicknamed Cheetah, and my mom was affectionately known as Dale. During these days we were living on Collington Avenue in east Baltimore. When I drive through the old neighborhood today, it still looks the same. The church on the corner with the large circular brick design stands out in my memory - it was a cornerstone of the community.

The human mind, a marvel of resilience, can cloak itself in a veil of oblivion, shielding itself from the harsh pangs of emotional turmoil. This protective mechanism, however, does not always extend to the radiant glow of cherished memories.

One such beacon of joy, etched indelibly in the corridors of my mind, is the recollection of a Christmas morning that stands as a testament to the transformative power of simple pleasures. As the first rays of dawn pierced the darkness, casting a warm embrace upon the snowy streets of Baltimore, I awoke to a sight that would forever be etched in my memory. It wasn't long before wrapping paper and scattered ribbons stretched across the living room floor, unveiling my magnificent spring ride rocking horse. Its sleek design and vibrant colors captivated me.

Accompanying this masterpiece was a cowboy outfit with two toy pistols that seemed to whisper tales of adventure. In this attire, I transformed into a fearless frontier marshal, ready to tame the Wild West, one gallop at a time on my spring-loaded rocking horse.

The echoes of laughter and the warmth of family love filled the air that Christmas morning, creating a tapestry of joy that would forever be woven into the fabric of my childhood memories. Pictures of that day, capturing the unadulterated happiness of youth, circulated for years, each a reminder of the simple pleasures that can make life truly extraordinary. Among these cherished images, one stands out: a photograph of my cousin Kim Lacks and me, our faces beaming with the unrestrained exuberance of childhood.

Memories of childhood fade in and out sporadically and sometimes seem random and without a chronological sequence. Shedding light on my memories help me to understand the man I've become today – life goes in a full circle.

My grandfather, David (Day) Lacks worked in the steel industry. It wasn't unusual for my mom to make my sister and I ride along when dropping him off at Bethlehem

Steel. It was a gigantic plant located at Sparrows Point in east Baltimore County, and dust was everywhere.

Mom always stopped at Logan Village Shopping Center to get a cheesesteak sub from Captain Harvey's Sub Shop. A single-sub sandwich had so much meat that it could feed 4 people. So, my mom would put a loaf of bread in the trunk to divide the meat between the entire family. She was a wise woman who knew how to stretch a little into a lot.

Druid Ridge Cemetery in Baltimore on Mother's Day 2019. Visiting the burial site of my mom, Deborah Lacks.

We moved to Alameda Village Apartments on Beaumont Avenue during my elementary years - my mom enrolled me in Northwood Elementary School. We lived near my mom's oldest brother, Uncle Lawrence, and his wife, Aunt Barbara (Bobbette). They had three kids: my cousins Ron, LaDonna, and Lawrence Jr.

A young Alfred Carter, Jr. in December 1972 at Fort Worthington Elementary School in Baltimore.

During this season, domestic violence started echoing through the walls as my dad attacked my mom. At that time, I held tightly to my spiderman sheets, unable to understand how two people who loved each other could argue, fuss, and fight so much. As I got older, I realized my dad was age 19, and my mom was only 17 when I was born, and having a child at such a young age was a new experience for them. Even worse, my dad's drug use created a considerable controversy.

My dad's side of the family was huge but less active in our lives than the Lacks. My Granddad Lee was a businessman who purchased and operated corner stores in east Baltimore from the 1960s to the 80s. My grandmother Mary Carter, nicknamed Lil Bit, was 4 feet 11 inches tall and 100 pounds soaking wet, and Granddad Lee was 6 feet 3 inches tall and 290 pounds. Mary managed to pop out 10 children for him, 7 boys and 3 girls.

My aunt Annie Mae lived in Detroit, Michigan, with her husband, Leslie, throughout my childhood. They had 4 children: Leslie Jr, Ann, Sharlana, and Kevin. Leslie retired from the Chrysler plant, and they visited Baltimore during the holidays in a huge mobile home. All the kids wanted to sleep in that camper.

Overall, I felt proud to be a Carter. Visiting our family-owned stores was special to me. Standing behind the counter with my Grandma Mary (Lil Bit) felt terrific. Three sisters came to the store to purchase chips and soda, and one of them was my childhood crush. Her name was Ronda, and she was so pretty. Ronda raced through my mind for a lifetime.

While my dad's family were business owners, the Lacks family were blue-collar workers and faced far more challenges. My mom had one sister, Elsie, who passed away in an institution at the tender age of 15 from epilepsy, and 3 brothers, Lawrence, David, and Joseph, who later changed his name to Abdul.

People called my grandad Day a "good man" and a hard worker. Granddad was a great provider. He kept nice cars until my uncle David, nicknamed Sonny, got his hands on them. Sonny dogged Granddad's cars before the new car smell was gone.

My cousin Lawrence Jr., nicknamed Cooch, and I, would always go with our granddad to the farm and pick fruits and vegetables. I remember a sense of freedom running in the open fields as an 8-year-old. I felt free from the urban air, the Baltimore hustle, and the domestic violence.

My granddad, who we called Pop, always had a liquor bottle and Donald Duck Grapefruit Juice. He smoked long, skinny brown cigarettes. Cooch and I would sneak one and go in the field and smoke it, trying to be like Pop. I'm convinced Pop knew, but we were the boys he loved so much he never said a word. He would always protect us from getting disciplined by our mothers, which consisted of "whoopings." "Leave those boys alone," Pop shouted. As a result, they'd put down their belts and pops words saved us from another harsh spanking.

After retiring from Bethlehem Steel in 1977, Pops received a white hard hat that my mother felt the need to get back from a beautiful woman named Brenda.

Brenda had a puzzling relationship with my Uncle Lawrence, and they had a daughter named Antonetta (Toni). Even still, they were our family. We never focused on the details of their affair, but Mom was furious about that hard hat. It was mainly because Mom felt she deserved it. After all, it was her dad, and she always took him to work, which made it difficult to understand how it got in Brenda's hands anyway.

It's the little things that meant so much to our family. Living in the shadows of such a great legacy and feeling the loss of her mom, Henrietta Lacks, made Deborah hold on to the simple things in life.

Brenda and her daughter, Antonetta "Toni", who is also my blood cousin and a member of the Henrietta Lacks descendants. This photo was taken in Baltimore, Maryland in the 1980's.

Deborah Jean Lacks aimed to protect Latonya and I from the negative nuances of Baltimore. From birth until now, I continue reminiscing about my limited childhood exposure, mismanaged options, and choices that caused me to spiral downward.

Chapter 3
REMINSCING

It's 8:35 a.m. **October 12, 2023**, and I'm reminiscing about how my life started on a downward spiral. Where did the root of my drug addiction start? Drugs, alcohol, and domestic violence changed the trajectory of my life as a child. I saw things that were not meant for kids to see, until my mother decided enough was enough.

As children, even at birth, our growth and development should be the responsibility of our parents. Our upbringing contributes to our behavior and character. If there is any dysfunction at all, chances are good that trouble will manifest and eventually cause a life of pain and suffering. I once read somewhere that "the teacher will appear once the student is ready." I am ready.

I've learned that my real problem did not lie in the drugs but in a distorted personality. My issues were further perpetuated by years of drug abuse. I am progressing as I face reality and grow stronger one day at a time. I'm now finding new meaningful interests that make my life feel fulfilling. I now realize that drugs only camouflaged my pain, disappointments, and frustrations.

Reminiscing has helped me identify powerful statements of self-awareness and growth. I recognize that drug abuse is often a symptom of underlying emotional or psychological issues. Digging deeply to address these issues is essential to a lasting recovery.

Unfortunately, some communities are stripped of resources, and many individuals have no support. As a result, they turn to drugs to cope with the complex realities that are too complicated to face alone.

Soon after, a distortion of personality occurs with drug abuse, and it manifests in many ways. For example, people who abuse drugs may develop unrealistic expectations of themselves and others. They experience a negative self-image and difficulty coping with stress and emotions. They suffer from impulsive behavior and difficulty forming healthy relationships.

I experienced all of these, and I know firsthand the disasters that happen when drugs are abused. These symptoms only get worse over time, and life only gets more complicated with drug abuse. Drugs only provide the delusion of a temporary escape from problems, but they ultimately make matters worse.

My daily confession is, "I am progressing as I face reality and grow stronger one day at a time." This is a testament to the power of recovery. It shows that even after years of drug abuse, it is possible to heal and reclaim one's life. My grandmother's immortal cells inspired me to believe that anything is possible. As a result, here I stand, set free from the consequences of poverty.

My mom, Deborah Lacks, made weekly routine visits to Alfred Carter while he was in prison at MCTC in Hagerstown, Maryland – this photo was captured in 2007.

I'm now finding new interests that mean something, and I now realize I was looking for fulfillment in drugs. Facing reality is a sign of a genuine and lasting recovery. It shows that we have found new, healthier ways to cope with stress and misplaced emotions.

I never knew my life had so much meaning until I decluttered my mind, gained a new perspective, discovered a sense of purpose, and learned new coping mechanisms to manage challenges. It was not easy redirecting a lifetime of misguided, misdirected, and mismanaged thoughts, but here's where my journey started.

First, I let go of my anger and resentment towards others. Secondly, I forgave myself for making mistakes in the past. Thirdly, I stopped dwelling on negative thoughts and memories. Fourthly, I focused on the present moment and appreciated the good things in my life. Fifthly, I learned to let go of things that I cannot control. Sixthly, I developed a more positive outlook on life. Seventhly, I learned to rely on God.

Everything I was going through as a young adult directly resulted from my childhood. I needed serious counseling and didn't even know it. During this season of my life, I was able to secure great jobs and connect with phenomenal women but lacked the tools to hold on to them. In some instances, I purposely sabotaged them without hesitation.

I was warned by my mom, Deborah Lacks, who was a strong woman of influence in my life. However, addiction is difficult, and I'd spiraled too low to recover without help. If you knew anything about my mother, you'd know she was determined and focused.

In the movie, "The Immortal Life of Henrietta Lacks" she was portrayed by actress, Oprah Winfrey. My mother diligently tried to dig up every detail about my grandmother. My mom spent years searching in the shadows trying to put history to the immortal cells of my grandmother, Henrietta Lacks. Most people are blessed with bright memories of their parents, but Deborah lost Henrietta before she was 2 years old. My mom spent a lifetime searching for her own identity in dark shadows.

Digging deep into my childhood memories while writing this book is sobering. It is a constant reminder that if I do not stay clean and abstain from drugs, I will undoubtedly return to the life of crime that once enveloped my entire existence.

The self-destructive behavior that I willfully participated in eventually led to a thirty-year sentence of first-degree assault, armed robbery, and use of a handgun in the commission of a felony. However, a series of events occurred before I ever found myself viewing the world from a prison cell.

Now that I'm stepping out of the shadows, I finally realize that telling my story sheds light in dark places. Giving voice to pain, shame, and disappointments is self-liberating. It also helps others with a blueprint to escape the pitfalls of poverty. Breaking free from the shadows means everything must come to the light. I've given it a lot of thought, and Grandma Henrietta would not want us walking in her shadows. So, I'm telling my own story and shining light on a way to escape the prison of marginalization.

Chapter 4
LIFE'S ROLLERCOASTER

On **January 22, 2016,** the day before the Baltimore blizzard of 2016, I was released from prison after almost 15 years. The 2-day snowstorm dumped 29.2 inches of snow in 2 days. I was thrilled and happy when I was granted a delayed release parole, and the day finally arrived.

Prison is a very difficult and unpleasant experience. It can be isolating, stressful, and even dangerous. Any ex-convict can tell you about the lack of privacy, lack of control, safety concerns, mental health issues, social isolation, and a sense of betrayal from many people on the outside. Contrary to what the system portrays, prison is not a place of rehabilitation.

Envision being confined to small, shared spaces, and told when to wake up, eat, sleep, and go to the bathroom. Picture dealing with the risk of violence daily, not only other inmates but also staff. Through the illegal access of contraband, a lot of people get exposed to addictive drugs while imprisoned. Stress in prison can lead to anxiety, depression, and post-traumatic stress disorder (PTSD). It's like getting used to living a nightmare. Of course, not all prisons are the same, but being locked up like animals is inhumane.

Some ill-informed people have a preconceived notion that having 3 hots, a cot, a TV, and periodic phone privileges is an advantage. It is by no means a wonderful and carefree life for an inmate, convict, detainee, or whatever other name society labels us. As sure as the beautiful sun rises in the east and sets in the west, prison is no way, shape, or form enjoyable.

For example, the three meals provided are miserably prepared, often served cold and cooked in roach and mice-infested kitchens. The portions are minimal enough to merely keep you alive. Most facilities force inmates to sleep on a steel plate slab with only a thin mattress that feels like a flimsy sheet. Even worse is the thought of it being reused by thousands of other inmates daily, year after year. There are no Sealy mattresses in prison.

The one thing readily available is time to adjust my mind and attitude and educate myself. During my years in prison, I consciously decided to take full advantage of every positive opportunity I would be exposed to upon my release. Unfortunately, prison disproportionately impacts people from lower socioeconomic backgrounds negatively. As a result, the bowels of this dark and dismal pitfall directly entrap Black people like me.

Statically proven, a high percentage of poor people are more likely to be arrested and convicted of crimes. Although I was guilty of the crime charged, I was innocent of the circumstances that created the mindset. Innocent people living impoverished communities are less likely to have access to the legal resources they need to defend themselves.

Therefore, those of us from lower socioeconomic backgrounds are more likely to receive stiffer penalties and longer sentences. The lack of financial resources force people to settle for court-appointed attorneys who specialize in negotiating a plea deal. Far too many inmates are victims of capitalism.

Most prisons offer a variety of courses disguised as rehabilitation programs, such as drug treatment, vocational training, and mental health counseling. However, these programs are often unavailable to lower socioeconomic prisoners. Chances are prisons in poor regions are overcrowded and have limited resources.

Due to these circumstances, people from lower socioeconomic backgrounds tend to re-offend after being released from prison. Recidivism, or repeat offending, is when someone who has been convicted of a crime commits another crime after they've been punished or served their sentence. It's a serious problem, with nearly half of all released prisoners ending up back behind bars within the first year.

This number jumps to two-thirds within three years and three-quarters within five years. That means that for every 100 people released from prison, 77 will be arrested for a new crime within five years.

These statistics are based on data from the National Institute of Justice, and they highlight the importance of helping former prisoners successfully reintegrate into society. They're much more likely to fall back into old patterns and commit new crimes without proper support.

These statistics alone is proof that prison is not a place of rehabilitation. Instead, people are merely confined and caged. Upon release, they are crippled by barriers to employment and housing – this is America's secret shameless epitome of marginalization.

Prison also impacts the families of those who are left at home. The negative impact on people from lower socioeconomic backgrounds can have a ripple effect. For example, when a parent is incarcerated, their children are more likely to experience poverty, neglect, and abuse. In my case, you'll soon learn how I lost my son to the streets. They are also more likely to drop out of school and become involved in criminal activity.

I was on home detention for 6 months while working at Jiffy Lube. During this time, I reconnected with my childhood sweetheart, Pastor Jewel, and a few months later, we married. As children, she was called Ronda – and Ronda was the jewel I met as a teenager working in Grandma Mary's (Lil Bit) store.

I passionately love my wife for who she is as a woman. Also, she can relate to me in so many ways. She's been through some of the same struggles I've experienced. We have so much in common, such as celebrating our father's birthdays, who were born on the same day, March 15th. Our paths crossed as teenagers when we attended the same junior high and high school. We made a spark in the 9th grade, and she became my high school sweetheart. Jewel and I grew up 2 blocks from each other. More than her tenderness and compassion, I admire her strength and determination, especially to do God's work.

Life can resemble a rollercoaster with many rapid ups and downs and unexpected twists and turns. It was May 12, 2009, when my mother, Deborah Lacks, died. It was the second time in my life that I cried. Having to listen to my mom's funeral services over the phone left me with tears of deep regret and unable to properly mourn her loss. After 15 years in prison, a lot had changed. Upon release, I started adjusting to my new reality, and finding emotional safety in Jewel's love.

On June 25th, 2016, amidst a gathering of cherished guests, we embarked on the most momentous journey of our lives – our wedding day. The air hummed with anticipation as we exchanged vows under the benevolent gaze of Bishop Shawn Bell, standing on a breathtaking 4.5-acre land generously provided by our dearest friend.

Alfred (Lacks) and Jewel Carter wedding on June 25, 2016, in Westminster, Maryland.

Wedding pictures with Keith Wainwright, Alfred Carter, Derrick Belton Jr. (The Ring bearer), and Trey Carter

Photo shoot for Pastor Jewel Carter's ministry on June 16, 2017, by Epic Media.

Reciting our wedding vows on June 25, 2016, in the presence of Ebony Phillips, LaTonya Carter, Darnesha Frazier, Alfred Carter III, Keith Wainwright, and Bishop Shawn Bell.

The sun cast a golden glow upon the jubilant faces of our beloved children - it felt like a dream to us both. Their presence was a testament to the enduring bonds of family. My son, whose life illuminated our world with joy, was a radiant symbol of hope and happiness. My sister,

LaTonya, with her heart brimming with love and pride, graced the occasion with her unwavering support.

As we strolled down the aisle, hand in hand, our hearts resonated with the soulful melodies of Indie Arie's "Purify Me." The song's lyrics echoed the profound transformation that was about to unfold, a union that would forever intertwine our destinies.

Surrounded by a constellation of close friends and family, we exchanged vows, our voices filled with the promise of a lifetime of love and devotion. Filled with wisdom and compassion, Bishop Bell's words blessed our union, setting the stage for a future brimming with shared dreams and unwavering commitment.

Alfred Jr. and Jewel Carter's first dance at their wedding.

The day unfolded like a tapestry of cherished moments, each one woven with threads of laughter, joy, and heartfelt blessings. The vibrant decorations, meticulously arranged by our thoughtful friend, transformed the venue into a sanctuary of love, reflecting the deep connections that bound us together.

As the sun dipped below the horizon, casting long shadows across the land, we bid farewell to our guests, our hearts overflowing with gratitude for their presence and well wishes. June 25, 2016, etched itself indelibly into our memories, an indelible mark of a day that forever altered the course of our lives. Jewel is genuinely my most precious jewel.

Alfred Jr. and Jewel Carter lighting a unity candle their wedding.

Alfred gazing into Jewel's eyes prepared to take their kiss as husband and wife.

Life's roller-coaster never stops but we must learn how to cope, even when it jumps off track. Two summers after our wedding, Jewel and I would share our most intimate connection. Gun violence in Baltimore City ripped both of our sons away from us. Jewel lost her son 20 years prior, and I lost my son the summer of 2020.

I begged my son, Trey, to follow my lead to legal success, but he insisted he could outslick the streets. My ex-wife and I had a strained relationship after I filed for divorce in prison in 2007. I felt like she abandoned me, and mother was my only support system. I had no plans on returning to anything or anyone who did not hold me down or mean me any good during while I was in prison. Being locked up like an animal changes the way you think about relationships.

Unfortunately, as an inmate, I was not able to provide my son with the fatherhood and guidance he needed and deserved. He turned to the streets and started peddling drugs. I loved him so much, but I failed him by making the decision that got me locked up when he needed me most.

The first time I cried, was September 16, 1996, when Trey was born. He was my namesake, Alfred Carter, III. The pride and joy I felt, the hope I saw, and the love I experienced embodied every entity of my existence and I wept. I wish I could have bottled up every tear to tangibly hold onto that moment forever. He looked like me and reminded me of the possibility of new beginnings. His birth made me feel immortal.

I was robbed of that feeling when Trey was mugged and murdered for $20,000. A piece of my soul died with him. The pain is indescribable. It was 5 days after his 24th birthday at 9:30 p.m. on September 21, 2020. This was the third and last time I cried.

During this time, the World Health Organization (WHO) declared COVID-19, a respiratory illness caused by the SARS-CoV-2 virus, a Public Health Emergency of International Concern on January 30, 2020.

The number of COVID-19 deaths globally remained high in September 2020. With 36,000 new deaths reported during the week of September 21st, I had tunnel vision because only one death mattered in that moment, my son.

The CDC predicted the US death toll to reach 200,000-211,000 by September 26. As of November 8, 2023, WHO reported over 6,985,278 deaths from COVID-19 globally. The pandemic prevented us from having a traditional funeral, with limited masked guests. Two of my dearests loved one's experienced burials under peculiar circumstances.

While the COVID-19 situation remained serious, vaccines and treatments helped reduce the severity. My grandmother Henrietta Lacks' HeLa cells were used as workhorses in the vaccine research. Ultimately, Henrietta Lacks' cells paved the way for the rapid development of life-saving vaccines.

HeLa cells' also contributions to medical advancements that go far beyond COVID-19 vaccines. Still, while my grandmother's cells saved the world, nothing could be done for Trey.

Perhaps one day I will mourn the losses of my mom and son properly, but the circumstances surrounding both their losses created too much frustration and anger for me grieve the way loved ones should.

Trey's murderers bragged about the money while displaying Trey's Louis Vuitton pouch on Instagram. Unfortunately, no one would testify against the murderer because in urban communities there's a no-snitch code.

My son, Trey, and my nephew Davon Meade paintball experience in Baltimore, August 2014.

The "no-snitch code" is an unspoken rule in some urban communities that prohibits individuals from informing law enforcement with details that lead to arrest. It is often rooted in a distrust of the police, a fear of retaliation from criminals, and a desire to protect one's own community.

In many urban communities, residents have experienced or witnessed police corruption, brutality, and racial profiling. The "no-snitch code" can also be seen as a way of protecting one's own community. In some cases, individuals may believe that informing on a criminal will lead to more violence or instability in their neighborhood. They may also feel they must protect their community, even if it means shielding criminals from punishment.

While the "no-snitch code" may be understandable in some contexts, it can have serious consequences. It can make solving crimes difficult, bringing criminals to justice, and protecting victims. It can also perpetuate a cycle of violence and mistrust. This is what happened in the case involving my son. No one would testify on behalf of Trey; criminals silenced our Baltimore community in fear.

Nonetheless, my mother always taught me that vengeance belongs to God. There were two criminals involved in my son's murder. Soon after, the first suspect was involved in a violent shootout. He was shot, captured, and caught on camera, initiating the violent crime. As a result, he was arrested and imprisoned.

The second suspect was killed in a motorcycle accident. I don't want hurt or harm to come to anyone, not is prison a place for Black men, yet I felt vindicated. The unspoken truth is that their consequences helped me avoid getting my revenge and facing more years in prison myself. It was test, and I put my trust in God.

The worst feeling in the world is knowing that I only had four years before going to prison and four years after being released to spend with my son. Life has been a rollercoaster, and Trey's death sent me spinning in circles, but I will always cherish those 8 years I spent with my only son.

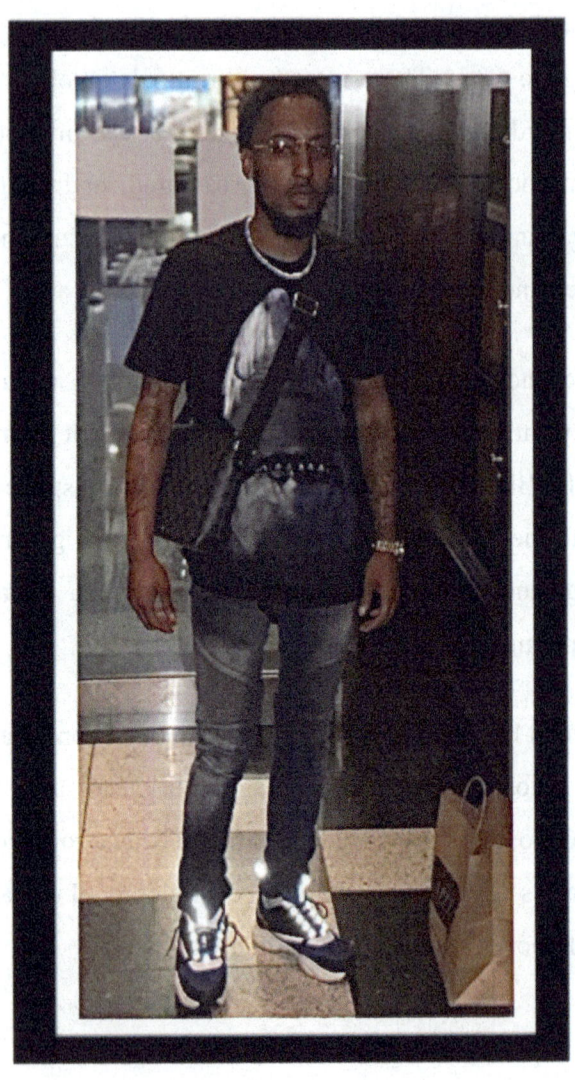

Alfred (Lacks) Carter, Jr. son, Trey Carter, III, on his 24th birthday, September 16, 2020, at Capitol Grille Restaurant, downtown, Baltimore. (He was murdered 5 days after this photo was taken).

Chapter 5
NO QUICK FIX

Upon release from prison, **January 22, 2016,** I released deep layers and complexities of urban inequalities. A complex web of challenges faces urban America's poorest citizens. As a result, there is no quick fix for several reasons, as Jonathan Kozol powerfully illustrates in his book "No Quick Fix." Here are some key aspects:

Firstly, intergenerational entrenchment is an obvious problem for marginalized people. Poverty isn't just a temporary setback; it's often a multigenerational cycle that creates a mindset within various urban communities. Limited access to quality education, healthcare, and secure housing traps families, making it harder for children to break free. Disadvantaged neighborhoods lack resources that middle-class children take for granted, perpetuating a cycle of limited opportunities.

Secondly, there are undeniable systemic barriers. Discriminatory policies and practices can create invisible walls, limiting opportunities based on race, ethnicity, or zip code. Independent resources show how zoning laws, school funding disparities, and unequal access to public services can concentrate poverty and hinder upward mobility.

Thirdly, there needs to be more comprehensive solutions - wealthy people don't understand the challenges, and poor people cannot grasp the solutions. Many existing programs address individual symptoms like hunger or homelessness. Still, there is a need to tackle the root causes like inadequate wages, exploitative lending practices, and limited social safety nets. My grandmother, Henrietta Lacks, clearly understood the need for holistic interventions that empower individuals. Poverty is a disease. As her descendent, I want to dismantle the systemic barriers while helping people overcome the symptoms of poverty.

Fourthly, political polarization is disastrous for marginalized people. Effective solutions often require collective action and long-term investments, which can be challenging. As a result of a politically divided climate, urban communities suffer the worst.

There is no magic wand, but urban America deserves a sustained effort, collective responsibility, and a deep understanding of low-income families' interconnected challenges.

When I was initially released from prison, I started doing speaking engagements to support Rebecca's book, "The Immortal Life of Henrietta Lacks." After 15 years in prison, I accepted any legal opportunity to gain a sense of stability. Looking back in retrospect, I have no regrets, but I would have done things differently with all I learned years after my release. Without question, if I could rewrite my life story, the narrative would be different from Rebecca's book.

Alfred Carter, Jr. and Alfred Carter, III at LAX airport 2016. Attending a speaking engagement at Charles Drew medical school

The movie, "The Immortal Life of Henrietta Lacks" was released in 2017. Oprah Winfrey's role as Deborah Lacks depicted my mother's character perfectly, as described in the book. Oprah met with my entire family, although she and I had a much closer relationship. On multiple occasions, we sat as friends over dinner, discussing her role as my mother. And she captured the essence my mother character on film.

Oprah Wintfrey meeting with the Lacks family along with Rebecca Skloot at the Four Seasons Hotel in Baltimore, Maryland in 2017.

Oprah helped me to establish my 501C3 non-profit, donating $100,000.00 in grants for my men's transitional house. She also asked the director to write a speaking part for me in the movie, which he did. My line was, "We're here to donate blood in case she needs it." It was a short role, but my first opportunity as a professional actor – and meeting Oprah was even more amazing. Oprah helped, inspired, and opened a door that allowed me to get on the right course in life.

Alfred and Jewel Carter in New York City on November 2019 for a speaking engagement at Suny Downstate Medical Center.

My focus as a free man is to continue my mother's story and my grandma's legacy. My cousins Veronica and Victoria and I are goodwill ambassadors for the World Health Organization for the elimination of cervical cancer. My uncle Lawrence was an ambassador until his death. He was an impressive man, retiring as one of the first African American locomotive engineers for Amtrak in Maryland.

I've traveled to Switzerland, Germany, Africa, Hawaii, and domestically, educating people on the importance of clinical trials, patient advocacy, cancer prevention and awareness, medical ethics, racism, and genetic justice for Henrietta Lacks. This is how my new beginning started.

Seventy-two years after the death of my grandmother, our family reached a settlement on August 4, 2023, in an unprecedented lawsuit for unjust enrichment. Attorney Ben Crump and his team of attorneys, along with Professor Deleso Alford and attorney Nigel Halliday helped us to reclaim our Lacks legacy. It is essential to our family to continue this fight because, for over 70 years, my grandmother's legacy and descendants were taken advantage of by the medical industry.

Our family is continuing to fight so everyone knows that Henrietta Lacks was a wife and mother of 5 young children when she was brutally mistreated and died at Johns Hopkins Hospital. Our attorneys, Ben Crump, Chris Seeger, Chris Ayers, and Nabehar Shaer, continue pursuing justice for

Henrietta Lacks. We are pleased with the recent resolution but ready to focus on our efforts to move forward in our fight for justice. We've written books, created fragrances, and stood up against multi-billion-dollar pharmaceutical companies.

There is no quick fix or easy solution, but raising awareness about cervical cancer and acknowledging the problems with our prison system is a start. However, it is vital to recognize the extent of the problem and to work to address its root causes. By addressing the socioeconomic inequalities that contribute to mass incarceration, we hope to help break the cycle of poverty and crime.

Chapter 6
A NEW BEGINNING

August 1, 1973, our next move was to 7258 McClean Blvd in Dutch Village. My mother always moved in the late evenings. She said, "The neighbors can't see what type of furniture we have if we move at night." Burglaries were common in Baltimore communities back then.

My mom's best friend, Valerie Ferguson, and her two daughters, Nettie and Kim, at Dutch Village town homes in Baltimore Maryland in 1980.

It was the house on the corner, which mom hated. Winter was rapidly approaching, and Deborah had a theory that the houses at the end of the block were more exposed to cold winds than those in the middle of street, which caused higher than usual heating bills. Winter temperatures in Baltimore get down as low as single digits and feels even colder as the wind whips through the neighborhood blocks. I remember shoveling snow as a child and putting on thick coats, gloves, scarfs, hats, and insulated boots to maneuver through the snow. Baltimore winters were bad.

Surviving the winters made us appreciate the summers even more. We had a patio out back and a neighborhood swimming pool close to our home. I learned how to swim at the pool and had my first fight with the bully on the block. I'd like to say the fight was a tie - nobody won - in my opinion. I was attending Yorkwood Elementary School, and my biggest dream was to be a crossing guard. I didn't have high hopes back then. More than anything, I wanted to wear the crossing guard badge of authority. Perhaps it was my deep desire to possess power, because life's situations in my home were beyond my control.

Also, I wanted a pair of shoes that were called rockers. I was interested in baseball, and the Orioles were my home team. My first year playing organized baseball was in

1973, and I was 7 years old. I was on the Loch Raven Giants, and we played at Mercy High School. I didn't have a clue what I was doing. I was new to sports.

Unlike our President at the time, the talented athlete Gerald Ford, I needed a lot more training at sports. President Ford played football for the University of Michigan, where he helped the team win national championships in 1932 and 1933. He was named the team's most valuable player during his senior year. Despite receiving offers from professional teams, Ford chose to pursue a career in law. When I was 8 years old, Ford became the 38th President of the United States. Anything is possible if you set your mind to it and stay focused.

During those days, my friends were Mike, Tudor, Kenny, Reggie, Teddy, Todd, and Tykie. Tykie told me his uncle, Willie Sturgill, played baseball for the Pittsburgh Pirates. Bruce was also my friend, and his mom was dating the son of the Baltimore Colts' head coach, Don Shula. Whether these stories were true or not, it made these guys really cool in our eyes. We were ordinary Black kids growing up in urban America. A personal connection to a professional athlete meant everything.

Overall, our home felt warm and welcoming. Our kitchen walls were off-white with yellow and blue borders. Brown wooden cabinets held all the canned foods mom stored. A spice rack, along with a large wooden spoon crossing over a matching fork was placed side by side as decorations on the wall. A decorative clock was positioned on the wall leading up the stairwell.

My mom worked two jobs: Gino's and Toys R Us. I had to watch my little sister and care for the house when she was away. My mom taught me how to clean the bathroom, wash and dry dishes, and mop the floor. She always said, "Alfred, mop the floor in sections so you won't miss anything." At the age of 8, Deborah taught me how to cut a whole chicken into parts and thread a sewing machine. Mom would sew her clothes with patterns from Epstein and Minnesota fabrics. She was a beautiful, domesticated, woman of faith with many skillsets.

During all the parental lessons, she managed to squeeze in uncomfortable talks about sex. She would tell me to always consider pleasuring my woman before trying to satisfy myself. My mother left no stone unturned.

My father, a man of bold strokes and deep hues, transformed our living room into a masterpiece of midnight elegance. An expanse of plush black shag carpet served as the canvas upon which he masterfully arranged his collection of midnight treasures. Like twin sentinels, a sleek black leather sofa and loveseat anchored the space, inviting one to sink into their depths and surrender to the allure of darkness.

Like fallen stars amidst the velvety void, scattered across the room were inviting black beanbags, promising moments of cozy solitude. A small bar, reminiscent of a speakeasy from a bygone era, adorned one wall. Suspended from the ceiling, a cascading net of fishnet draped the room like a shimmering waterfall, adding an element of intrigue and mystery to the décor.

Upon the table, a "thinking man" statue hinting at the depths of my father's intellect and the weight of his thoughts. A love knot, painted in vibrant shades of crimson and gold, adorned another wall, its intricate twists and turns symbolizing the enduring bond between my parents. And on yet another wall, a poster of my mother and father, captured in a moment of timeless love. These decorations were a constant reminder of the foundation upon which our family was built.

My father's living room was more than just a space to gather; it reflected his soul, a testament to his affinity for the bold and the beautiful. It was where shadows danced, secrets whispered, dreams took flight, and imaginations soared. It was a world of his own creation, a place where one could escape the mundane and immerse oneself in the artistry of darkness.

He also illuminated everything with a psychedelic purple glow. I recall my father's friends gathering around his component stereo, listening to rhythm and blues. Laughter and mingling saturated the room with the haze of marijuana smoke. Sometimes, he'd even blow the smoke into my face, leaving me with a lingering, unsettling sensation. When my mother discovered this incident, it marked the final straw. Without hesitation, she summoned the police and had him evicted from our home, never to return. It was the final straw, and understandably so.

This transition profoundly transformed our lives. As the eldest, I assumed the role of the man of the house, taking on the responsibility of caring for my younger sister. Mom, understandably, was acutely aware of our vulnerability and instilled in us a deep sense of safety. She emphasized the importance of never leaving food unattended on the stove, a rule we followed without question.

Opening the door to strangers was another strict no-no, a consequence of the vulnerability we had experienced. Mom's concerns extended to fire safety, and she meticulously instructed us on how to evacuate our home in the event of a blaze. We learned to feel the door for heat, a crucial step in determining whether it was safe to exit. Crawling to safety was another essential skill she imparted, emphasizing the importance of staying low to avoid smoke inhalation.

My mother and grandfather would often engage in heartfelt conversations about my grandmother, Henrietta. Mom was barely two years old when Henrietta succumbed to cervical cancer in 1951. A yearning to understand her mother better burned within Mom and Pop would patiently delve into Henrietta's remarkable story. He would explain how Henrietta's cells, known as HeLa cells, possessed an extraordinary ability to thrive and reproduce endlessly. Mom, filled with a sense of awe and fascination, showed me a genetics textbook featuring a chapter dedicated to her mother's unique cells. Seeing one of my family members immortalized in a scientific publication was a remarkable experience.

We eventually had to move again because even though Dad lived with his girlfriend, Gwen, he would still get drunk and come by to terrorize Mom. Banging on the front door and belting out profanity. Dad would be drunk and high, yelling, "I'm going to beat yo' ass." Scared out of my mind at this recurring abuse, his threats spiraled through my mind day and night. I feared for my mother.

Like Black Lightening, the darkness would always disappear before the cops came. I was 10 years old and in the sixth grade, already dealing with instability as a kid. Soon after, Mom met her new boyfriend, Roosevelt, a truck driver. He drove a 1976 brown Plymouth Duster, and his CB handle was Moon Duster. We moved in with him and his 2 sons, Charles, 17, and Gregory, 10, just like me. We lived in a 3-story brick home in northeast Baltimore.

Roosevelt, hailing from Farmville, Virginia, where his aging father still resided and tended to his farm, became a constant presence in our lives. Occasional trips to Virginia marked our calendar, offering us a glimpse into his roots. Roosevelt, a man with a kind heart, carried the burden of an alcohol addiction. Yet, he never treated my mother or us with disrespect. Their love for each other was evident, and he genuinely welcomed us into his family, extending his warmth to my sister and me.

After two years, my mother decided to part ways with Roosevelt, citing personal reasons - reasons I may never understand. Once again, we packed our belongings and embarked on a new chapter, leaving behind the sense of family and the friendships I had passionately cultivated.

The year was 1978, and we moved to Garden Village. I stepped off the bus at 6021 Lanette Road, my new home address. I enrolled in Golden Ring Junior High School, my seventh school, and I was only in the 7th grade. Mom worked as a lab technician for Genstar, a rock quarry.

Me and my teammates at the 2023 Nationals for 40 and over. Three peat champions Towson baseball league from Towson, Maryland.

Determined to leave the instability of my past behind, I threw myself into sports, playing baseball and football for

Gardenville. Sports became my lifelong outlet. My hard work paid off, and I quickly became a standout player, leading my teams to championships in baseball and football. I'd finally gotten the hang of athletics.

My time at Golden Ring was a transformative experience. Amidst the challenges of a new school and home, I found solace and purpose on the playing field. Sports taught me the importance of teamwork, discipline, and perseverance. These are lessons that would stay with me long after graduation. As I look back on my time at Golden Ring, I am grateful for the opportunities it provided. I discovered my passion for sports there and learned the values that shaped my life in the long run.

My sister LaTonya was on the cheerleading squad with the other girls from our neighborhood, and once again, I made friends. This time it was Trevor, Mike, Joe, Lamont, and Butch, to name a few. We formed bonds and played together, and fixed and built bicycles. It was 1979, marked by Rapper's Delight storming the airways with rap music. I had a few girlfriends, Debbie, Rozzie, Chantel, and Ramona, but I lost my virginity to Charlene.

Alfred Carter, Jr. and my sister LaTonya Carter at 2718 East Biddle Street, at my paternal grandmother's house, Mary Carter, the summer of 1971.

It was such a surreal moment for me that I remember it like yesterday. I felt a sense of freedom - I was growing up fast. Having a bicycle and good friends gave me a sense of liberation whenever we left our neighborhood. The guys and I listened and laughed at Richard Pryor's albums in Lamont's basement. Unfortunately, these were the years when I first tried marijuana. We were eager to be adults, and barely knew enough to be functional children.

By 1980, I experienced a time of societal shifts and personal transitions. Amidst this backdrop, my mother, a woman of unwavering strength and resilience, embarked on a new chapter in her life. She met James, a man of faith and conviction, and their paths intertwined, leading to a union in 1981.

James, a preacher by vocation, carried an aura of authority and an unwavering commitment to his beliefs. Sundays became a regular pilgrimage to St. Stephen's church in Essex. In this sanctuary, the echoes of hymns and prayers filled the air. My sister and I, eager to embrace this new chapter, joined the youth choir.

Initially, James's presence exuded a sense of order and structure, a welcome change from the uncertainty that had often characterized my childhood. Though strict, his rules seemed to provide a sense of stability, a much-needed anchor in life's ever-shifting currents.

However, as time unfolded, James's rules tightened like the grip of a rattle snake without warning. His attitude caused a dark shadow to drift over the initial warmth and acceptance I'd previously perceived. I spent my entire childhood walking in other people's shadows. Each day, his grip grew firmer, his demands becoming increasingly inflexible. The man of the house, a role I had once proudly held, was gradually usurped by this new figure, who commanded obedience rather than fostering the camaraderie of loving-kindness I had once known.

Our relationship felt forced. The title "Pop," which James insisted I use, felt like an ill-fitting garment, a label that failed to capture the essence of the grandfather – the man I will always cherish as Pop. James' demeanor was devoid of the warmth and understanding. I associated nothing about him with my grandfather. With each sunrise and every sunset, James left me with a growing sense of alienation.

As the oppressive weight of James's authority intensified, my spirit rebelled, yearning for the freedom and autonomy I had once enjoyed. I longed to break free from the shackles of his rigid rules and expectations.

Despite the growing tension in our household, my mother remained a steadfast pillar of strength, her love and affection an unwavering hope amidst the raging storm. She stood as a fortress, shielding us from the full brunt of James's sternness.

With each passing day, a new chapter unfolded, a journey of self-discovery and understanding. We sought to unravel the complexities of James's character, to decipher the man behind the preacher. In the quiet moments, when words were scarce and emotions ran deep, we glimpsed the vulnerabilities beneath his stern demeanor.

We realized that James's strictness was a misguided attempt to shield us from the harsh realities of life, a misguided manifestation of his protective instincts. His rules and demands, though flawed in execution, stemmed from a genuine desire to safeguard our well-being.

Even still, the instability of my upbringing had taken its toll, and the repressed emotions that had festered for years began to erupt. My frustration, anger, and loneliness manifested in a pattern of misbehavior. James and I clashed constantly, his criticisms highlighting my perceived shortcomings. The frequent school changes had left me feeling abandoned and adrift, contributing to my withdrawn nature and emotional instability.

Mom and James (Pop) bought a house at 5604 Frankford Ave in 1982, and she was thrilled to buy her first house. After years of relocating her kids from house to house, she finally owned a home. Halfway through my 10th-grade year of high school, Pop and I could no longer co-exist. We almost came to blows. Many years later, while I sat in prison, my mother and James divorced, about 2 years prior to her death.

Meanwhile, Mom asked Uncle Lawrence and Aunt Barbara (Bobbette) if I could finish high school while living in their home. At this point, I was using marijuana to smoke away my problems almost daily, and life consisted of going to school, getting high, eating, sleeping, and having sex. I was disconnected from reality.

I played football and was on the wrestling team during my senior year - perhaps these sports helped to release my aggression. I graduated high school and immediately afterward enlisted in the Marine Corps. For 4 years, I started out great, living in California and North Carolina. Unfortunately, things were not great emotionally nor resolved mentally. My unstable childhood had taken a toll on me. I took my drug habits into the military, where it caused me to go AWOL and eventually get a bad conduct discharge in 1986. But my story did not end there. I kept spiraling downward.

Alfred (Lacks) Carter, Jr. and Lisa Ann Pinchback at Baltimore City College Preparatory High School senior prom in Baltimore, Maryland, May 1985.

CHAPTER 7

ABSENT FROM GOD'S PRESENCE

At 10:45 a.m., **November 1, 1986,** I faced the consequences of my actions after going AWOL (Absent Without Leave). Going AWOL from the military can lead to severe consequences, depending on the circumstances. AWOL is considered a serious offense that can result in various punishments. It's a scary feeling to have racing thoughts about what criminal penalties the government will impose, not to mention the monetary fines.

In addition to these formal penalties, I had to deal with several informal consequences of going AWOL. It damaged my reputation and job opportunities, and it caused serious financial troubles. I hoped I would only get reprimanded, but it was far more complicated.

While I was in the brig, my 1985 Nissan Stanza was loaded on a tow truck and repossessed. It felt like everything was being taken away from me. Returning to Baltimore, I stayed with my uncle Lawrence again, going from job to job trying to find employment while also trying to find my self-worth. My instability with jobs and relationships led me into a deeper hole.

I spiraled into the allure of the white powdery substance like a siren's call, beckoning me into a sea of addiction. My first encounter with the substance was like a warm embrace, a comforting illusion of safety and security. It was as though all my problems had faded away. It enveloped me in a cocoon of euphoria, shielding me from the harsh realities of life. I was lost in this false paradise, oblivious to the treacherous path I was treading.

As the years unfolded, I found myself trapped in a relentless cycle of addiction, my life spiraling downward like a leaf in a hurricane. The substance, once a source of fleeting pleasure, became my master, dictating my every move and enslaving my will.

My descent into the abyss was marked by shattered dreams and broken promises. I was a prisoner of my own making, held captive by the very thing I had sought solace from. In 1988, the harsh reality of my choices came crashing down. I was arrested again, this time for selling cocaine. My actions kept catching up with me like a vengeful ghost. The weight of my transgression settled heavily upon my shoulders, a crushing burden that threatened to consume me entirely.

The consequences of my actions were swift and severe. I was sentenced to probation. The shackles of the law bound me, forcing me to confront my demons. The next four years were a blur of struggle and despair. I held down a series of menial jobs, but I lost each one due to my growing grip of illegal drugs. I was in denial, delusional, and dysfunctional.

Marijuana is arguably called a gateway drug. Every user will not move on to use more addictive substances. However, many people feel the urge to try something stronger that will get them higher for longer periods than marijuana. I'm not proud of my choices back then, but heroin soon became my drug of choice. Heroin is an insidious parasite that latched onto my soul, sucking the life out of me. It drained me of everything that mattered and left me feeling like a hollow shell of emptiness - nothing mattered.

Consider a whisper promising escape, a gripping hug from the shadows of nowhere. This is the deceptive allure of heroin, an illegal opioid drug born from the poppy's embrace. Its beauty is a lie; its touch is a venomous kiss. This white or brown powder, sometimes a dark, sticky tar, is morphine's twisted offspring. It floods your brain with euphoria, a stolen moment of bliss. But like a predator offering a poisoned treat, heroin demands a heavy price.

Addiction is a tightening grip that squeezes the air from your lungs and steals your will. The final chapter for many is defined by an overdose, a closing curtain that falls without warning. I was one of the lucky ones. Heroin is not a friend, not a lover, not even a fleeting high. It's a wolf in sheep's clothing, a predator in paradise. Its touch is ruin, its kiss a lethal dose of oblivion. Remember, it whispers a deadly lullaby. Heed the silence before the music starts, the darkness before the light fades.

With each snort of the white powdery substance, I sought to escape the torment of my existence. It was a temporary escape, but I was attracted to the deceptive illusion. It was like a cruel mockery of the true peace I desperately needed. The substance promised peace but delivered torment. I was lost at sea; my life drifted in raging waters of my own making.

There are other detrimental effects of heroin addiction that can lead to harmful behaviors, such as risky sexual practices. I discovered that having sex high on heroin felt fascinating. It made me feel like a porn star with staying power for hours. For years, my addiction made me think I was escaping pain, guilt, and shame. Still, really, I was digging myself deeper into a tunnel of becoming a functional addict.

Heroin use creates such a heightened sexual experience, but it comes at a significant cost. Heroin addiction is a chronic and debilitating disease that can have devastating consequences on a person's physical, mental, and emotional well-being. It even leads to a range of health problems. Thankfully, I did not overdose, suffer from organ damage, or get infectious diseases. However, my addiction strained relationships, ruined my employment record, led to criminal activity, and stole years of my life.

I was no longer in control - entirely dependent on a drug. I soon became self-centered, and my priorities were all messed up. I was a bad person, treating others like they had no value because I had no self-worth of my own. I bounced from job to job and woman to woman. It was as though I was oblivious to my disease of addiction - drugs will blindside you. I lost my girl Kathy and was in and out of jail for theft, shoplifting, and other misdemeanors.

I received a 4-year sentence in 1992 from Judge Byrnes; little did I know he was saving my life. I did 10 months at Herman L. Toulson boot camp in Jessup, Maryland. I thought I had my addiction under control. Still, I did not educate myself and started dipping and dabbing.

Being absent without leave (AWOL) is the same as being absent-minded and addicted to heroin. These are the same situations that spiral downward when you are absence from God's presence. I was detached from reality and disregarded life's responsibilities. My euphoric highs and lows were colliding, and I found myself plunging deeper into a self-inflicted cycle. My detachment issues started breeding neglect, leading to a cycle of repeated consequences affecting every area of my traumatized life. My memories were scattered, bouncing back and forward from adulthood and childhood, tragedy to triumph, and feeling lonely to falling in love.

CHAPTER 8
FROM BOYS TO MEN

On **July 8, 1995**, things began to turn around for me. I worked for my aunt Daisy at her liquor store when I met Sharon. She became the mother of my only son in 1996, and we married in 1999. My sobriety from 1993 to '99 paved the way for my job as a conductor/engineer for CSX Transportation.

Family photo with my uncle Lawrence Lacks, his daughter Donnie, her daughter Erica, aunt Barbara, my granddad Day, my mom Deborah, and uncle Sonny, taken at 1304 Kitmore Road, Baltimore, Maryland in the 1990's.

I knew God's hands were on my life when I got hired at CSX Transportation as a conductor in 1995. I'd just got fired from my job as a machinist. My cousin Ron asked me to go with him to take the CSX test. It was the third and final day they were testing and accepting applications.

Out of 8 thousand applicants, they hired seven people. Even as a convicted felon for drug charges, I was one of the 7. My cousin didn't get an interview, and to this day that memory seems to impact our relationship.

I presented myself well and interviewed exceptionally and got the job. Two months later, I was in Cumberland, Maryland, training to familiarize myself with the railroad. A career in the railroad industry can be both challenging and rewarding. It offers a variety of job opportunities, from train operators and conductors to track maintenance workers and engineers. The work is often physically demanding and requires long hours, but it also provides opportunities to travel, work outdoors, and be part of a team. I had not felt like a team player since high school.

There are many pros and cons to working on a railroad. On the positive side, railroad jobs are relatively secure, pay well, and offer opportunities for advancement. There is also a variety of work to choose from, and some railroad workers have travel opportunities. However, the work can be physically demanding, with extended hours and irregular shifts. It can also be stressful, as the railroad industry is highly regulated.

Railroad workers can thrive in the industry with proper training, education, and a commitment to safety. My training included the locomotive's mechanical, electrical, and air brake components. Also, we learned how signal lights, colors, and positions defined safety signals. Our training required an understanding of railroad signal systems and interpreting their indications. We had to be familiar with the different types of railroad signals, their color schemes, and the meanings of the various signal aspects. My job gave me a sense of purpose and self-value. I was finally back on track - literally.

I was a conductor traveling from Baltimore to Philadelphia, Richmond, Virginia, and Cumberland, Maryland. My job included reading work orders and assisting engineers when coupling or uncoupling train cars. A few years after getting hired, I attended engineering school in Atlanta, Georgia. Railway engineering programs provide a comprehensive education in railway system design, construction, operation, and maintenance. Students in these programs gain a strong foundation in the principles of railway engineering, including track geometry, railcar dynamics, and signaling systems.

We also learned about transportation planning and modeling, track mechanics, railway electrification, railway safety management, and railway economics and finance. Graduates of railway engineering programs are well-prepared for careers in various industries, including freight rail, passenger rail, transit rail, railroad consulting firms, railway equipment manufacturers, and government agencies.

Would you believe it? After everything I'd been through, I was now operating locomotives; it was a great job and paid well. An engineer could make more than $100,000.00 a year back then, which was a lot of money. Not knowing enough about my drug addiction, I allowed the pressure and stress of work and life, along with my newly earned financial resources, to slowly cause me to relapse. I was caught in a cycle and no matter what good thing happened in my life, I managed to destroy it.

Like freight cars coming apart, things started falling apart from the seams. Locomotives typically fall off the tracks for three reasons: track defects, equipment failure, and human error. My mistakes were a combination of all three. Defects in my life and damaged ties eventually resulted in the loss of my job.

Loss is the act of misplacing or failing to find something. It is the state of not having something you used to have. Loss is the harm or disadvantage that results from losing something or the decrease in the amount or value of a thing. Loss creates a feeling of sadness or grief caused by the loss of something or someone. I've experienced a lifetime of losses, but remained convinced that one day I would win.

Unfortunately, my dad passed away from mesothelioma in 1999, and because I was not educated, healed, or in a healthy place, I relapsed. Once again, my life deteriorated fast. Afterward, I immediately got my Commercial Driver's License (CDL) and began driving garbage trucks for the next two years. Until my friend Eric and I made a miserable decision that sent our lives spinning in circles.

The transition from boys to men is a multifaceted process encompassing physical, emotional, and social changes. It's not a single event but a gradual journey shaped by individual experiences and cultural contexts.

It's important to remember that individual experiences vary significantly as we go from boys to men. Some boys may transition faster or slower, and their journeys may be influenced by factors like race, ethnicity, socioeconomic status, and family dynamics.

Ultimately, transitioning from boys to men is about cultivating a sense of self, developing emotional maturity, taking responsibility, and forging meaningful connections with others. It's a lifelong process filled with challenges and triumphs, but ultimately, it's about becoming the best version of yourself.

I was almost 30 years old, pretending to be a man, but I had not fully gone through the transition. I was still trying to cope with all the injustices I'd experienced in life. I suffered from the lack of stability, the trauma of seeing domestic abuse, the loss of loved ones and the inability to grieve properly, manipulation, drugs, divorce, and losing my son to murder in the streets of Baltimore. I needed to know that my pain had a purpose. I was desperate to dance with justice. When transitioning from boys to men, you learn that the cliché is true, "No justice, no peace. "

CHAPTER 9

JUSTICE FOR ALL

On **August 26, 2023**, my Uncle Lawrence Lacks passed away, one month after the first Henrietta Lacks settlement. It was victorious moment for our family. I think he lived to see justice for his mother.

We lost my uncle Lawrence at the age of 88; he was the last living child of Henrietta Lacks. Lawrence Lacks, Sr., was also her eldest child. He was born in his mother's beloved Clover, Virginia. As a young boy, he with his family to the Turner Station community in Baltimore, Maryland.

Lawrence fondly remembers waking up and the whole house smelling like fresh-baked bread. It was the intoxicating aroma of Henrietta's soulful cooking.

He also laughed when describing how she used to chase after him for giggles and laughter. Playing as a boy and spending his days swimming was how he described his care-free life in the presence of Grandma Henrietta.

Lawrence was only 16 years old when his mother, Henrietta, suffered a rapid and painful death from metastatic cervical cancer in the "colored ward" of Johns Hopkins Hospital in 1951. Lawrence would have to mourn her passing while helping with his younger siblings, David "Sonny" Lacks, my mom Deborah Lacks, and Joseph (Zakariyya) Lacks.

Uncle Lawrence and Aunt **Bobbette** also took my mother in when she was pregnant with me at the age of 16. My mom fished high school. It would be 16 years later, and I would do the same.

More than two decades later, Uncle Lawrence and his wife Bobbette learned that the unique cancer cells responsible for his mother's death had been harvested without permission.

These cells were acquired from Henrietta's body, cultivated in a Johns Hopkins laboratory, distributed to researchers around the world, and kept secret from the Lacks family. These "HeLa" cells launched a multibillion-dollar industry. While my family remained proud of the scientific advancement made possible by the blood of Henrietta, the disservice was heartening. We all felt the pain of being exploited and misused as marginalize people of color.

The August 5, 2023, settlement announcement at Canton Water Park in Baltimore, featuring Ron Lacks, Alfred Lacks, attorney Ben Crump, my wife, Jewel Carter.

To lead our family in reclaiming our story, Uncle Lawrence co-authored *HeLa Family Stories*, in which he shares his firsthand descriptions of daily life with his mother, Henrietta. Uncle Lawrence gives a vivid picture of the woman who brought HeLa cells to the world. Unfortunately, the stories of African Americans are rarely heard or publicized unless told through the lens of Anglo-Saxon perspectives.

There is a long list of African American stories told by white people and made famous. The exhaustive list starts with early literature, such as "Uncle Tom's Cabin" by Harriet Beecher Stowe in 1852 and "The Birth of a Nation" by D.W. Griffith in 1915.

However, this concept flourished even more in modern literature. In 1932, "The Light in August" by William Faulkner. In 1976, "Deep River" by Alice Walker was criticized for its romanticization of slavery and its lack of historical accuracy. In 2009, "The Help" by Kathryn Stockett tells the story of Black maids in Jackson, Mississippi, during the Civil Rights era.

The book and the movie "The Blind Side," written by Michael Lewis in 2006 and adapted into a film by John Lee Hancock in 2009, continue to receive criticism. "The Blindside" is the story of African American NFL player Michael Oher, who contested its accuracy. He claims the film exaggerates his learning disabilities and downplays his existing football knowledge. He also alleges the Tuohy family, portrayed as benevolent saviors, exploited him financially and took advantage of him. The movie is also criticized for oversimplification of complex issues, clichéd characters and plot, and inaccuracy of events.

Even the 19th-century minstrel performances featured white entertainers in blackface singing and dancing to racist stereotypes. While famous then, they are now recognized as harmful and offensive. It's important to note that this list is not exhaustive, and there are many other examples of African American stories appropriated by white storytellers.

The popularity of these stories speaks to the complex power dynamics of race in America and the need for critical examination of how these narratives have shaped our understanding of Black identity and history.

To be clear, not all stories told by white people about African Americans are problematic. The act of using White storytellers is not inherently bad. However, we must be aware of the power dynamics at play and ensure that stories are told with sensitivity and respect for the lived experiences of the communities being represented.

There is a growing movement of African American storytellers reclaiming their narratives and sharing their experiences in their voices. This is an important step towards dismantling harmful stereotypes and promoting a more accurate and inclusive understanding of Black history and culture.

As a family, Henrietta Lacks descendants learned this the hard way. What we had to say in books about our own family fell on thorny ground. Yet, when Rebecca told a culturally insensitive narrative about our family, it was published and produced as though it was better soil. However, that will not stop me from echoing the shadows of immortality.

Uncle Lawrence and Aunt Bobbette's book also depicts the struggles of our family. The descendants that Henrietta Lacks left behind as they worked to overcome the trauma from medical racism, injustices, and abuse endured for decades.

Lawrence founded the family-led foundation honoring his mother's legacy. He was actively advancing his family's HELA100: The Henrietta Lacks Initiative as an advisor, speaker, and historian who has traveled the world to share his invaluable insights with global leaders, students, researchers, and community leaders.

In 2021, Lawrence proudly led his family in visiting the World Health Organization (WHO) headquarters. We went to Geneva, Switzerland for a special dialogue acknowledging Grandma Henrietta's contribution to revolutionary advancements in medical science.

It was a moment of justice. He honored his mother with a W.H.O. Director-General's award, recognizing her world-changing legacy. In 2022, Uncle Lawrence was named a World Health Organization Goodwill Ambassador for Cervical Cancer Elimination.

You cannot escape justice. It is not a lazy dog napping in the sun. It's a tireless wolf, always on the prowl. You can sprint through sun-dappled fields or hide in moonless caves, but justice will find you.

Justice isn't just a destination; it's a journey woven into the very fabric of reality. It might arrive dressed in the golden sunrise, bearing a crown of wildflowers for kind hearts and helping hands. Or, justice could emerge with fury, like a bloodthirsty wolf for its next prey for those who sow shadows and reap tears. So, choose your path wisely because justice will follow, painting your world with its own vibrant hues, whether in sunlight or storms.

Even still, some people think they can outrun justice. I was one of those clueless people. I had a "catch me if you can" mentally. Sunny days made me believe I'd escaped the shadows of my past.

CHAPTER 10
CATCH ME IF YOU CAN

March 19, 2001, the sun was shining brightly, casting a deceptive glow over the gritty streets of Baltimore, Maryland. The city, once known for its vibrant charm, had lost its luster, earning itself the grim nicknames "Badmore," "Murderland," and "Harm City." The former mayor's optimistic slogan, "The City That Reads," seemed a cruel mockery of the harsh realities plaguing us here.

Baltimore, the city I was born and raised in, was a grim tapestry of despair. It held the dubious honor of leading the nation in murder, violent crime, teenage pregnancy, HIV infection, and unemployment. The city was drowning in a sea of drugs, their insidious grip tearing families apart and leaving lives in shambles. Some people escaped, others survived, a few are still waiting to be rescued, and others drowned. I was no stranger to this darkness.

My own life had been ensnared in the city's underbelly, a victim of the very forces that ravaged Baltimore's soul. As I walked through the shadows of the deserted streets that day, the weight of the city's burdens pressed heavily upon me. The air was thick with the smell of desperation, seeping into our very pores.

I felt a surge of anger, a righteous fury directed at the powers-that-be who had allowed my city and my life to crumble. Their negligence, apathy, and greed paved the way for Baltimore's downfall. They had failed us, their constituents, their fellow human beings.

Amidst the despair, a flicker of hope remained. I knew that Baltimore was not beyond redemption. Like my grandmother, Henrietta, once vibrant and resilient, the city's spirit had not been wholly extinguished. It lay dormant, buried beneath layers of hardship and neglect, but it was still there, waiting to be rekindled.

I vowed that day to play my part in Baltimore's revival. I would not let my city be defined by its darkest hour. I need to do something, starting with telling my truth. I'm standing up for marginalized people whose voices have been imprisoned - not with bars, but by systems of discrimination.

I plan to write a new chapter for Baltimore, a chapter filled with promise and resilience.

I remember when I had my first encounter with hope. Life as a married man with a toddler son was a whirlwind of responsibilities. My ex-wife Sharon, 5'8" tall, with a thin build and brown skin, had a sharp tongue and often smoked Newport cigarettes. She was two years my senior. Despite being married for two of our seven years together, happiness was a rare visitor in our household.

My son, Trey Carter in Baltimore City on May 2014.

Our family was a motley crew. Trey, our four-year-old son, barely beginning his of passage of transitioning from a boy to a man. He inherited his father's good looks and his mother's intelligence. This combination made him a force to be reckoned with.

Ebony (Woo), my 17-year-old bonus daughter, was a typical teenager, more interested in boys and late-night phone calls than schoolwork. Woo was a good kid at heart. My most significant responsibility was to my family. It was a weight I carried through the jungle of Baltimore daily - I had to ensure they ate by any means necessary. So, I hauled the city's trash.

The 1995 big, stinky green trash truck rumbled down the narrow east Baltimore alley, its groaning engine echoing off the brick walls and iron fences that lined the tight passage. I gripped the steering wheel, my hands steady despite the bumpy ride and the constant barking of dogs from behind the fences. Inches to spare on each side, Donnell, my trusty co-worker, guided me back, yelling loudly, "Come on back!"

My eyes locked on the mirrors, watching my crew tossing the neighborhood's trash into the compactor. The smell of garbage saturated the air, a pungent mix of rotting food, old coffee grounds, used baby diapers, and the lingering scent of last night's party. People's lives lay bare in their trash, a story told in discarded packaging, crumpled receipts, and the remnants of their daily routines. You could tell a lot about someone by what they threw away.

"Pack it, Al!" Donnell's voice echoed, and I pressed the button to engage the blade, its powerful thrust sending the trash cascading into the truck's belly. The truck groaned under the weight, its hydraulics straining to compress the growing pile of waste.

I was a CDL trash truck driver, a silent observer of the city's underbelly, and a witness to my fellow citizens' daily habits and hidden lives. My truck was a rolling time capsule, collecting the debris of our existence, the tangible evidence of our lives. As I maneuvered the truck out of the alley, I couldn't help but wonder about the stories behind the trash and the lives that unfolded behind closed doors and fenced-in yards. I was a part of the city's rhythm, its invisible pulse, clearing away the debris of our daily lives, making way for the new.

As we rounded the corner towards the end of the alley, Donnell and Henry, my trash-collecting comrades, hopped back into the truck's passenger side, their movements swift and practiced. Henry, a dark-skinned man with an athletic build and gold-rimmed glasses, settled into the middle seat. "What's the plan, y'all?" I asked, my eyes scanning the remaining four alleys on our route.

Henry glanced at his watch. "It's only 9:40 a.m.," he replied, his voice laced with a hint of apprehension. "Resco's (the incinerator) gonna be packed by now." Donnell nodded in agreement, his face etched with a mix of impatience and discomfort. "Yeah, let's get our blast now," he said. "I'm not trying to sit in that line feeling dope sick." My stomach churned by the mere mention of drugs, but I managed to keep my expression neutral. "Cool," I replied, trying to sound nonchalant. "I heard they got a bomb on Milton and Hoffman." We used street language that non-users wouldn't comprehend.

The truck lurched forward as I pressed the accelerator, the rhythmic rumble of the engine masking the tension in the air. Henry and Donnell fell into an animated discussion about the quality of the heroin they'd heard was circulating, their voices a low murmur that I tried to ignore.

I focused on the task of driving, navigating the narrow streets of east Baltimore, my mind a whirlwind of conflicting thoughts. I was a trash collector, a man of the streets, yet I found myself caught in the undercurrents of the city's drug culture.

The conversations about heroin, the references to dope sickness, they were all too familiar, a constant reminder of the dark side of the city I called home. As we pulled up to the corner of Milton and Hoffman, I felt a wave of unease wash over me. I wanted to escape the snare of my addiction, but it took on a life of its own. It's like I was possessed. I was dependent on each fix, desperate for dope, yet living life as a functional addict.

The neighborhood was known as a hotspot for drug activity, and the sight of loitering figures and illegal exchanges did little to calm my nerves. "Alright, here we go," Donnell said, his voice suddenly tight with anticipation. I nodded silently, my heart pounding in my chest. We were about to enter the lion's den, stepping into a world where addiction ruled, and desperation reigned supreme.

After copping our fix of heroin, we headed back to the route to complete our job and then went to Resco to dump the truck. "Man, you're a driving motherfucker," Henry said. I maneuvered the big green funk box on wheels in and out of traffic like I was driving a Volkswagen Beetle.

I replied, "Nigga, you know I'm the shit behind the wheel. I can drive anything that moves. It runs in the family." I smiled and remained focused, despite my fix. Glancing to my right, I now see Donnell in a full nod, feeling the effects of the smack. Paying attention to the road and traffic around us, I can't help but think that my life isn't so good right now. I worked every day to pay our bills, and I pulled illegal side hustles to support my drug habit.

"Donnell," I shouted! "Wake the fuck up, we back at the yard." He came out of his nod, talking to himself. His eyes were bloodshot red with a sliver of slobber escaping the left corner of his black crusty lips. He said, "Nigga I ain't sleep. I was just resting my eyes." We all exploded in laughter. The Mack truck whipped into the first available parking spot up against the fence. I killed the engine and removed the key as we left work, and I went to face my family.

On my way home, my phone rang, and it was my friend and accomplice. He's a tall, lanky guy who's lost weight due to his drug use. I answered the call and asked him what was up. We had robbed a store together the previous week, and he was still rattled from the experience. "Al, where the hell are you," he asked urgently, his voice laced with fear? "I'm on my way home from work," I replied. "Why? What's wrong?"

"Dude, the police have my picture on TV!" he said. I was completely lost and had a lot of questions. "What? Who took pictures," I asked, confused and concerned. "The cops who moved me and Kevin last week got us on camera," he explained with a trembling voice. "I didn't even see any cameras there!" I told him he needed to leave his mother's house immediately, as that would be the first place the police would look for him. I instructed him to meet me at our friend Gerald's house, and I would be there in 15 minutes. He agreed and hung up the phone. As I drove to Gerald's, I was speeding, and my mind was racing with ways to handle this situation - I felt reckless and high.

I parked my car one street over from Gerald's block, attached my gun to my belt, and walked through the alley. I reached the basement back door, tapped the window, and saw Eric peeping out the window.

"Open the door, you scared ass nigga," I said, smiling. "So, where are you going?" He replied, "Down to Atlanta with my cousin." While moving from the back of the basement to the front, I noticed far too many people in the house using drugs who would snitch with no regard. "Get your shit Eric, and let's get the fuck out of here," I said.

After gathering all his drug paraphernalia, we scattered. Rushing through the alley to go unnoticed, we finally reached my car and hopped in. Placing the key into the ignition, I looked over at Eric, and his panic-stricken face showed a hint of relief as he reclined into the soft leather seat of my Toyota Avalon.

As I pulled from the parking space, genuinely concerned, I asked, "Are you ok?" Right hand over his eye, secretly wiping away tears of fear, Eric replied, "Shit, I've been better." A counterfeit smile stretched across his lips. Only in extremely intense and stressful circumstances would I allow smoking in my car, and this was one of those situations.

My homeboy, Eric, is wanted man with his picture on TV for armed robbery. "Shit, that has to be at least 15 years," I thought to myself. Reaching inside the armrest, I grabbed my pack of Newport Kings, lit one up, and passed it to Eric.

As we cruised through the neighborhood, the bleak reality of a wounded Baltimore unfolded before our eyes.

Every corner housed a display of desperation: young men hawking their illegal merchandises in hushed tones, mothers barely teenagers carrying the weight of the world on their hips, addicts *stumbling* like the living dead, and women offering their bodies for chump change. I'd ghosted a woman named Donna after cheating on my wife with her, and guys were yelling loudly, "Bro, Donna looking for you." Guilt of my infidelity echoed in the streets. Just one journey down those streets brought us face-to-face with despair, painted in glaring and unforgiving strokes.

As Eric and I rolled to a stop in front of my house, an unsettling feeling came over me, an intangible shadow I couldn't quite pin down. Stepping out of the car, I reached for the bag stashed in the backseat, my mind still a whirlwind of anticipation and uncertainty.

Suddenly, a stealthy green Nissan, Maxima emerged from the gloom, inching towards us like a phantom predator. I initially thought it was a buddy dropping by to collect the DVDs I'd borrowed the previous week. But as the car glided past, revealing an unfamiliar license plate, my heart lurched into overdrive.

In the blink of an eye, the Maxima stopped, its presence casting an awkward sense of fear over the scene. And then, as if summoned by some unspoken cue, four more cars materialized, their crimson brake lights glowing in the darkness.

Eric and I, on high alert, scanned our surroundings, an uneasy feeling creeping up our spines. In that split second, a menacing convoy of cars with darkened windows suddenly raced up our street, screeching to a halt and forming a tight circle around us. The air crackled with tension as cops emerged, their faces grim and their guns drawn, their voices echoing with urgency, "Get down on the ground! Now! Get down on the ground!"

With my hands raised in surrender, I couldn't help but feel the pain of regret for Eric. I'd tried to get him out of Baltimore to the safety of Atlanta, but the long arm of the law had reached him just the same. The arresting officer, a white man in a worn-out T-shirt, sneakers, and an

Orioles cap approached me. His face was grim, his eyes cold and hard. "Alfred Carter," he said, his voice a low growl, "you're under arrest."

My mind raced, trying to piece together the puzzle. "Which crime could this be," I thought to myself? I'd made my share of mistakes and taken my fair share of risks, but which one had finally caught up with me? The weight of my past actions pressed down on me, a suffocating burden that threatened to crush my spirit.

An overhead helicopter with searchlights brighter than the midday sun descended upon the scene, casting an eerie spotlight on the crowd of curious neighbors. Suddenly, an epiphany struck me like a bolt of lightning. Those random cars I'd noticed over the past month weren't figments of my paranoid imagination; I was under surveillance. Even our house phone, which I meticulously avoided using for illicit dealings, bore the unmistakable marks of being tapped.

The Baltimore County robbery unit, hot on my trail for the previous month's store robbery, had finally closed in. As detectives swarmed my house, searching every nook and cranny for guns and the fruits of my ill-gotten gains, Eric and I found ourselves facing the cold, hard reality of our actions. My actions finally caught up with me.

My wife and son stood frozen on the sidewalk; their eyes wide with disbelief as I was led away in shackles. I locked gazes with them, my heart heavy with love transcending the iron bars that would soon separate us. "I love you both," my voice thick with emotion. "Everything will be alright." Seeing my son's tears streaming down his cheeks like raindrops shattered my composure. The pain and fear etched on Sharon's face mirrored the turmoil in my own soul.

As I was shoved into the back of the police cruiser, my voice echoed, "Sharon, let everyone know I'll be back. Put the house up for bail." Her shoulders slumped, her eyes mirroring the defeat in her voice, she uttered, "It's not possible. We don't have the equity."

For the first time, a lifetime of missteps crystallized into a harsh reality I'd been desperately evading. I was trapped, a man on a slow-motion march towards a thirty-year prison sentence, a mere ghost of my former self, haunted by the question of how my life had veered so irreparably off course.

Chapter 11

THE IMMORTAL TRIUMPH

It was **August 2, 2023**, when everything started coming full circle. After 72 years of waiting and two years of fighting against the pharmaceutical industry, we won our first settlement. Yet, this is not the end of our legacy. The immortal life of my grandmother is a symbol of hope for all people who have been marginalized, belittled, discriminated against, or exploited.

Our legacy is an enduring testament to the inherent value of every human life. Human dignity is a cornerstone of our existence regardless of race, ethnicity, past mistakes, current struggles, failures, or personal beliefs. This absolute truth transcends all boundaries. It took the medical community 72 years to recognize Henrietta Lacks' family.

After decades of using her cells to profoundly impact medical advancements, we received a belated acknowledgment of our inherent worth. Yet, we continue to persevere, unwavering in our commitment to uphold the dignity of every human being. Our journey is far from over. We are guided by the steadfast belief that everyone possesses the right to be treated with compassion, respect, and fairness. We will continue to champion the cause of human dignity, ensuring that the legacy of Henrietta Lacks resonates throughout generations, inspiring a world where every human life is valued and celebrated. We will continue fighting the good fight of faith.

Let this book serve as a resounding reminder that my grandmother, Henrietta Lacks, was born with the name Loretta Pleasant on August 1, 1920, in Roanoke, Virginia. Her parents were Eliza and Johnny Pleasant. When she was a young girl, her mother passed away, and she went to live with her grandfather, Tommy Lacks, on a tobacco farm in Clover, Virginia, a place she loved dearly. Eventually, her name was changed from Loretta Pleasant to Henrietta Lacks. In 1941, she married my grandfather, David "Day" Lacks, in Halifax County, Virginia.

As a young mother, she moved north with my grandfather, Day, to find better opportunities in Baltimore. They moved to the Turner Station neighborhood of Dundalk, Maryland. Day and Henrietta built a life for themselves and their five children:

Lawrence, Elsie, David, Deborah, and Joseph (Zakariyya).

Alfred Carter, Jr. and my grandfather David "Day" Lacks, September 19, 1999. My first wedding to my son's mom in Baltimore.

Grandma Henrietta was renowned for her unwavering compassion and commitment to helping those in need. She had an uncanny ability to identify individuals within the community who were struggling, particularly those who had recently moved to the city in search of manufacturing jobs. With open arms and a warm heart, Grandma Henrietta extended a helping hand to these marginalized individuals, providing them with food, essential resources, and valuable connections. She established a beacon of hope, fostering a supportive network for those seeking to rebuild their lives and find their footing in Baltimore.

My family affectionately called her "Hennie." Throughout her life, Grandma Henrietta was an extraordinary woman whose heart overflowed with love for God, her husband, her children, her community, dancing, cooking, horseback riding, and fashion. She was as radiant and full of life as her favorite color, red.

My grandmother's legacy extends far beyond the HeLa cells that have revolutionized medical research. She was a beacon of compassion, tirelessly caring for those around her while quietly battling her pain. In 1951, at the tender age of 31, Henrietta's life was tragically cut short by cervical cancer. Despite valiant treatment, the disease swiftly ravaged her body. Unbeknownst to her grieving family, this tragic loss marked the dawn of a medical revolution, as her cells, unbeknownst to her, had already embarked on an extraordinary journey.

Visiting Grandma Henrietta's gravesite in Clover, Virginia, August 1, 2022. Cousin Ava Flood, cousin Bria Baptiste, wife Jewel Carter, cousin Victoria Baptiste, Alfred Carter Jr., Uncle Lawrence Lacks sr., and cousin Veronica Spencer.

Just hours before Henrietta's final breath, scientists at Johns Hopkins Hospital, the institution where she had been treated, revealed a groundbreaking discovery – the world's first immortal human cell line, HeLa, derived from Henrietta's cervical tissue without her knowledge or consent.

While the medical community celebrated this scientific breakthrough, our family remained shrouded in the dark shadows of their loss. We were unaware of the remarkable legacy Grandma Henrietta had unknowingly left to humanity, her cells tirelessly multiplying and replicating, fueling medical advancements that would touch countless lives. Yet somehow the lives of her descendants were left dangling in despair.

As the HeLa cells continued to proliferate in laboratories worldwide, we struggled to make ends meet, unaware of the immense value of the cells taken from our family. It wasn't until decades later that we learned of Henrietta's extraordinary contribution to medicine. This discovery brought both pride and a sense of injustice.

Henrietta Lacks' story is a poignant reminder of the power of human cells and the ethical dilemmas surrounding their use in medical research. Her legacy lives on not only in the countless lives touched by the HeLa cells but also in the ongoing debate about informed consent, patient rights, and the equitable distribution of the benefits of medical advancements.

From the depths of Henrietta Lacks' cancerous tumor emerged a miracle, a testament to human resilience – the HeLa cells, named after the first two letters of her name.

These miraculous cells, born from Henrietta's adversity, would revolutionize medical research, becoming the first immortal human cell line capable of replicating indefinitely in a laboratory.

Alfred (Lacks) Carter, Jr. posing at my grandmother's walk of fame star downtown Baltimore on September 2017; Located at Corner of Mulberry Street and Howard Street.

Unbeknownst to our family, her cells were multiplying, yet their impact echoed across the globe. These remarkable cells, capable of thriving outside the human body for over 36 hours, fueled groundbreaking medical advancements, unlocking the secrets of cancer, viruses, and countless other ailments.

While the HeLa cells transformed the world of medicine, our family remained shrouded in the dark. Her extraordinary legacy was hidden from us. For two decades, Henrietta's cells, numbering in the millions, were commercialized and distributed worldwide, fueling the engine of modern medical progress.

It wasn't until 1975, over two decades after Henrietta's untimely passing, that her family would uncover the truth about her cells, their remarkable resilience, and their profound impact on humanity. The revelation was a bittersweet symphony, a blend of pride and injustice, as we grappled with the knowledge that Grandma Henrietta's cells had transformed medicine without our knowledge or consent.

The world would never be the same after the "HeLa" phenomenon began in 1951. The HeLa cells are continually used for research and to test theories about the cause and treatment of diseases. Over 50,000,000 metric tons of HeLa cells have been distributed worldwide and reproduced billions of times to become the subject of more than 75,000 studies.

The medical miracle of Henrietta Lacks. Photo taken at Turners Station in Maryland, during the Late 1940's.

Even though HeLa Cells launched a multi-billion-dollar industry for human biological materials, our family had not received any of the revenues. Henrietta Lacks' prolific cells grew for seven decades and contributed to remarkable medical advances. HeLa cells contributed to Nobel Prize-winning developments of the polio vaccine, the discovery of human papillomaviruses (HPV) causing cervical cancer and the later creation of the HPV vaccine, the discovery of the human immunodeficiency virus (HIV), research on telomeres, and advances in live viewing of cellular growth. Most recently, HeLa cells contributed to the 2021 Nobel Prize awarded discovery of receptors for temperature and touch.

In addition to the study of treatments for the effects of cancer, hemophilia, leukemia, and Parkinson's disease, HeLa cells have been used in research that has contributed to understanding the effects of radiation and zero gravity on human cells.

HeLa cells have been credited for creating the field of virology and were vital for the "omics" revolution, from genomics to transcriptomics and proteomics. From informing research on chromosomal conditions, cancer, gene mapping, precision medicine, and even the current coronavirus studies as the world responds to the COVID-19 pandemic, Henrietta Lacks' HeLa cells continue to help save lives. Unquestionably, HeLa cells are a miracle.

Henrietta Lacks, a name forever etched in the halls of medical history, unwittingly transformed the world with her extraordinary cells, now immortalized as the HeLa cell line. There is no other known human being whose cells have been able to live outside the body. There was something divine, undying, and immortal about Henrietta Lacks. She was an extraordinary human being that continues to marvel scientist and physicians worldwide.

Hailed as the "Mother of Modern Medicine," a "Heroine of Modern Medicine," a "Medical Miracle," and a true "Wonder Woman," Henrietta's legacy has transcended borders, inspiring countless individuals and igniting a global movement to honor her impact.

Henrietta's story has been immortalized through countless memorials, conferences, museum exhibitions, libraries, and print and visual media. Author Rebecca Skloot captured Henrietta's remarkable journey in her New York Times bestselling book, *"The Immortal Life of Henrietta Lacks,"* which later inspired an HBO FILMS movie adaptation starring Oprah Winfrey. Unfortunately, her narrative reflected poorly and inaccurately when describing Black cultural experiences.

Ben Crump and Alfred Crump at the March 14, 2022, SEALS conference at Southern university in Baton Rouge, Louisiana.

From the halls of the United States Congress to state legislatures and local policymakers, Henrietta's profound contributions have been recognized and celebrated. Her legacy has also resonated globally, earning her honors from governments, artists, schools, universities, scientists, patient advocates, social justice leaders, and countless others.

Even today, Henrietta Lacks continues to touch lives in ways many may never realize. Her rich history and extraordinary legacy are a source of pride for her family and a cornerstone of modern bioethics policies and informed consent laws that safeguard patient rights and foster trust in the medical community.

In a landmark 2013 agreement, the Lacks family partnered with the medical, scientific, and bioethics communities to forge the groundbreaking HeLa Genome Data Use Agreement, granting us the authority to oversee and regulate the HeLa genome sequences and discoveries. This unprecedented collaboration marked a pivotal moment in ensuring that Henrietta's legacy is honored and respected, ensuring that her contributions continue to benefit humanity for future generations. Even as marginalized people, we, the grandchildren of Henrietta Lacks, were finally being heard.

In 2020, Henrietta Lacks' 100th birthday was commemorated worldwide with the launch of HELA100:

Henrietta Lacks Centennial CELLebration. It was a year-long initiative spearheaded by The Lacks Family. This momentous year also witnessed the World Health Organization and the National Women's Hall of Fame, further solidifying Henrietta's global legacy. The Henrietta Lacks Enhancing Cancer Research Act was signed into law in the United States on December 18, 2020.

This crucial legislation mandated a study by the U.S. Government Accountability Office. As a result, federal agencies are now addressing the barriers in federally funded cancer clinical trials for underrepresented populations.

Marking Henrietta Lacks' 101st birthday in 2021, The Lacks Family announced the advancement of their philanthropic initiative, "HELA100: The Henrietta Lacks Initiative." This endeavor aims to educate future generations about the impact of Henrietta Lacks' HeLa cells while promoting health equity and social justice. To commemorate 70 years since Henrietta Lacks' HeLa cells revolutionized the world and her untimely passing on

October 4, 1951, The Lacks Family embarked on a groundbreaking journey with the HELA100 Worldwide Tour.

Henrietta (Hennie) Lacks

On October 4, 2021, the HELA100 Worldwide Tour commenced in Bristol with the unveiling of a life-size statue of Henrietta Lacks. This historic sculpture, commissioned by the University of Bristol, is the first public representation of a Black woman created by a Black woman in the UK. The tour continued throughout the UK and extended to Germany, where our family

Alfred and Jewel on a European tour with the Iris team in Hamburg, Germany on October 8, 2021.

We are driven by an immortal bloodline that inspires us to stand for marginalized people. Other books have been written about my grandmother, such as *"HELA Family Stories"* by Lawrence and Bobbette Lacks and *"Henrietta Lacks, the Untold Story,"* by Ron Lacks, and others.

We will uplift Grandma Henrietta's contributions to the world from generation to generation. The Lacks family is transitioning from victims to victors with a proud family heritage.

We are grateful to everyone who has taken the time to learn about Henrietta Lacks, our family, and her HeLa cells. Always remember, the immortal cells of Henrietta Lacks are a gift that keeps on giving.

We will continue to spread our positive message to schools, libraries, associations, communities, and organizations worldwide, ensuring that Henrietta Lacks' contribution to humanity is never forgotten.

SHADOWS OF IMMORTALITY

For Speaking Engagements and More Information About:

The Untold Struggles of Henrietta Lacks' Grandson

Contact:
Alfred (Lacks) Carter, Jr.
Phone: 443-864-1145

E-mail:
ShadowsofImmortality23@gmail.com

Made in the USA
Coppell, TX
09 August 2024

35768828R00085